a little taste of...

thailand

a little taste of...
thailand

Recipes by Oi Cheepchaiissara
Photography by Alan Benson
Additional text by Kay Halsey

MURDOCH BOOKS

contents

SPECIAL FEATURES

limes and lemon grass **16**   noodles **34**   *phrik* (chillies) **52**
tom (soups) **72**   *yam* (salads) **84**   curry pastes **110**
naam phrik (chilli sauce) **128**   shrimp paste and fish sauce **160**
rice **180**   coriander, basil and mint **204**   the coconut **230**

a little taste...

The food of Thailand is startlingly bold and imaginative. Carefully crafted to appeal to all the senses, it combines beautiful presentation with fragrant aromas, contrasting yet complementing flavours and textures, and often fearsome chilli-heat.

Although Thai food appears unique, it is in fact one of the world's great fusion cuisines. The country may never have been colonized, but Thai chefs certainly absorbed foreign influences. As in much of Asia, Chinese culinary ideas are very strong, particularly in the form of noodle dishes, soups and techniques from stir-frying to steaming. Indian spices give fresh-tasting Thai curries their deeper, toasty notes, while the flavours of Southeast Asia are tasted in satay and coconut curries. Even infamous Thai chillies are not indigenous, but were introduced by the Portuguese in the sixteenth century.

Thai cooks, many of them attached to the royal court, transformed these new ingredients and techniques into something distinctly Thai by combining them with ancient seasonings: the basic flavourings of garlic, pepper and coriander (cilantro) root; fresh-tasting lemon grass and pungent Thai herbs; sour makrut (kaffir) lime and tamarind; galangal, Asian shallots and garlic; sweet coconut and palm sugar and salty fish sauce and shrimp paste.

These flavours are not, by any means, subtle, but Thai cooking blends them into graceful dishes where no one taste overpowers the others. Above all, Thai cooks value balance, and it is the combination of sweet, sour, salty and hot tastes that makes the food vibrant. With seasoning so important, it is no surprise that the mastery of Thai cooking lies in the labour-intensive creation of its curry and soup pastes, which contrasts strongly with the cuisine's quick cooking techniques.

Although to the western palate take-away noodles from a street stall may seem a decent lunch, the Thais consider it a meal only if it is enjoyed with family or friends and eaten with rice. A meal typically combines a soup, relish, curry, a fish, meat or vegetable dish and a salad, all of which are served at once so that the careful complementing and combination of flavours, textures and presentation can be appreciated. With so many strong, complex flavours, a few spoonfuls of just one dish at a time are taken to eat with the rice.

This may be Asia, but chopsticks are used only for Chinese dishes — for anything else, a spoon and fork are provided. In true Thai style, few rules govern the table; instead the emphasis is on friendly hospitality and a shared enjoyment of the food. When all the dishes have arrived, the hostess will announce *'kin khao'*, 'eat rice', and the meal begins.

a little taste of...

Among Asia's great snackers, the Thais only really eat one main meal a day; everything else is considered a snack. No shopping centre or hotel is without a stallholder frying crispy corn cakes, no busy *soi,* or lane, is free from vendors skilfully slicing green papaya salad, and some streets are practically open-air restaurants. A trip to the market is not just to fill your basket with the freshest produce, but a chance to cruise the food stalls, picking at hot charcoal-grilled satay or pandanus-wrapped parcels of chicken. And Thailand's night markets are justly famous for their specialities, serving flash-fried noodles out of pushcart kitchens from 6 pm to 6 am.

   The most remarkable thing is just how memorable Thai hawker fare is. In few places in the world can a wok on a street corner produce such wonderful food, and dishes like *Phat Thai,* which are almost always eaten as a snack, are best made on the sidewalk. Each vendor specializes in just one kind of cooking, sometimes in just one dish, and the results can be magical. Hawker food is always traditional, carefully prepared daily for an enthusiastic Thai audience who knowledgeably search out the best.

...hawker food

chicken satay

1 kg (2 lb 4 oz) skinless chicken breast
   fillets

MARINADE
2–3 Asian shallots, roughly chopped
4–5 garlic cloves, roughly chopped
4 coriander (cilantro) roots, finely chopped
2.5 cm (1 inch) piece of ginger, sliced
1 tablespoon roasted ground coriander
1 tablespoon roasted ground cumin
1 tablespoon roasted ground turmeric
1 teaspoon Thai curry powder

2 tablespoons light soy sauce
4 tablespoons vegetable oil
410 ml (1^2/$_3$ cups) coconut milk
2 tablespoons palm sugar
1^1/$_2$ teaspoons salt
40 bamboo sticks, about 18–20 cm
   (7–8 inches) long
peanut sauce (page 251) or cucumber
   relish (page 251), to serve

Makes 40 sticks

Cut the chicken fillets into strips 4 cm (1½ inches) wide x 10 cm (4 inches) long x 5 mm (¼ inch) thick and put them in a bowl.

Using a food processor, blender or pestle and mortar, blend or pound the shallots, garlic, coriander roots and ginger to a paste. Add the paste to the chicken, along with the ground coriander, cumin, turmeric, curry powder, light soy sauce, vegetable oil, coconut milk, sugar and salt. Mix with your fingers or a spoon until the chicken is well coated. Cover with plastic wrap and marinate in the refrigerator for at least 5 hours, or overnight. Turn the chicken occasionally.

Soak the bamboo sticks in water for 1 hour to prevent them from burning during cooking.

Thread a piece of the marinated chicken onto each stick as if you were sewing a piece of material. If the pieces are small, thread two pieces onto each stick.

Heat a barbecue or grill (broiler) to high. If using the grill, line the tray with foil. Barbecue the satay sticks for 5 to 7 minutes on each side, or grill (broil) for 10 minutes on each side, until the chicken is cooked through and slightly charred. Turn frequently and brush the marinade sauce over the meat during cooking. If using the grill, cook a good distance below the heat. Serve hot with peanut sauce or cucumber relish.

450 g (1 lb) firm white fish fillets
1 tablespoon red curry paste (page 245)
  or bought paste
1 tablespoon fish sauce
1 egg
50 g (2 oz) snake beans, finely sliced
5 makrut (kaffir) lime leaves, finely
  shredded
peanut oil, for deep-frying
sweet chilli sauce, to serve
cucumber relish (page 251), to serve

Makes 30

Remove any skin and bone from the fish and roughly chop the flesh. In a food processor or a blender, mince the fish fillets until smooth. Add the curry paste, fish sauce and egg, then blend briefly until smooth. Spoon into a bowl and mix in the beans and makrut lime leaves. Use wet hands to shape the fish paste into thin, flat cakes, approximately 5 cm (2 inches) across, using a tablespoon of mixture for each.

Heat 5 cm (2 inches) oil in a wok or deep frying pan over a medium heat. When the oil seems hot, drop a small piece of fish cake into it. If it sizzles immediately, the oil is ready.

Lower five or six of the fish cakes into the oil and deep-fry them until they are golden brown on both sides and very puffy. Remove with a slotted spoon and drain on paper towels. Keep the cooked fish cakes warm while deep-frying the rest. Serve hot with sweet chilli sauce and cucumber relish.

For a variation, make up another batch of the fish mixture but leave out the curry paste. Cook as above and serve both types together.

fried fish cakes
with green beans

stir-fried noodles with holy basil

**450 g (1 lb) wide fresh flat rice noodles
(*sen yai*)**
2 teaspoons soy sauce
4 garlic cloves
4 bird's eye chillies, stems removed
4 tablespoons vegetable oil
**200 g (7 oz) skinless chicken fillets,
cut into thin strips**
2 tablespoons fish sauce
2 teaspoons palm sugar
½ bunch (1 cup) holy basil leaves

Serves 4

Put the noodles in a bowl with the soy sauce and rub the sauce through the noodles, separating them out as you do so. Pound the garlic and chillies together with a pestle and mortar until you have a fine paste.

Heat the oil in a wok and add the garlic and chilli paste and fry until fragrant. Add the chicken and toss until cooked. Add the fish sauce and palm sugar and cook until the sugar dissolves. Add the noodles and basil leaves, toss together and serve.

limes and lemon grass... The incredible aroma of a steamy bowl of *tom yam* says much about Thai food. One of its distinctive characteristics is the use of fresh seasonings to impart a lemony essence and floral flavour. In Thai cooking, garlic and shallots, along with the aromatic root seasonings of ginger, turmeric and peppery galangal, are the foundations of many dishes. Fish sauce and shrimp paste add a salty taste, chilli some heat, and coconut and palm sugar bring sweetness. But it is the sour yet refreshing citrus notes of lime and lemon grass that balance the dish.

Although Thai cuisine is often described as lemony, in fact, lemons don't grow at all in the tropical climate. Instead, the juice of small, sour Thai limes is often added to cut the sweetness and oiliness of dishes. Alternative sources of that characteristically sour Thai taste come from tamarind or vinegar. The bitter juice of the makrut (kaffir) lime is rarely used in Thai cooking, but its leaves and bumpy rind are used for their musty, limey fragrance, as are chunks of lemon grass, bruised with the back of a cleaver to release oils and yet more fragrance into curry pastes and broths.

400 g (2 cups) corn kernels
1 egg
3 tablespoons rice flour
1 tablespoon yellow curry paste
  (page 246)
2 tablespoons chopped Asian shallots
1 tablespoon fish sauce
25 g (½ cup) roughly chopped coriander
  (cilantro)
1 large red chilli, chopped
peanut oil, for shallow-frying
cucumber relish (page 251), to serve

Makes 8

Combine the corn kernels, egg, rice flour, curry paste, shallots, fish sauce, coriander and chilli in a bowl. Shape the mixture into small patties, adding more rice flour, if necessary, to combine into a soft mixture.

Heat the oil and fry the corn cakes for 3 to 4 minutes, turning once, until golden brown. Serve hot with cucumber relish.

sweet corn cakes

chiang mai noodles

PASTE
3 dried long red chillies
4 Asian shallots, chopped
4 garlic cloves, crushed
2 cm (¾ inch) piece of turmeric, grated
5 cm (2 inch) piece of ginger, grated
4 tablespoons chopped coriander
   (cilantro) roots
1 teaspoon shrimp paste
1 teaspoon Thai curry powder

5 tablespoons coconut cream
2 tablespoons palm sugar
2 tablespoons soy sauce
4 chicken drumsticks and 4 chicken
   thighs, with skin and bone

500 ml (2 cups) chicken stock or water
410 ml (1⅔ cups) coconut milk
400 g (14 oz) fresh flat egg noodles
chopped or sliced spring onions (scallions),
   for garnish
a handful of coriander (cilantro) leaves,
   for garnish
lime wedges, to serve
pickled mustard greens or cucumber,
   to serve
roasted chilli sauce (page 250), to serve
Asian shallots, quartered, to serve

Serves 4

To make the paste, soak the dried chillies in hot water for 10 minutes, then drain and chop the chillies into pieces, discarding the seeds. Put the chillies in a pestle and mortar with the shallots, garlic, turmeric, ginger, coriander roots and shrimp paste and pound to a fine paste. Add the curry powder and a pinch of salt and mix well.

Put the coconut cream in a wok or saucepan and simmer over a medium heat for about 5 minutes, or until the cream separates and a layer of oil forms on the surface. Stir the cream if it starts to brown around the edges.

Add the paste and stir until fragrant. Add the palm sugar, soy sauce and chicken pieces and stir well, then add the stock and coconut milk and bring to the boil. Reduce the heat and simmer for 30 minutes or until the chicken is cooked and tender.

Meanwhile, cook 100 g (3½ oz) of the egg noodles by deep-frying them in very hot oil in a saucepan until they puff up. Drain on paper towels. Cook the remaining noodles in boiling water according to the packet instructions.

Put the boiled noodles in a large bowl and spoon the chicken mixture over the top. Garnish with the crispy noodles, spring onions and coriander leaves. Serve the accompaniments alongside.

225 g (8 oz) finely chopped prawns
   (shrimp)
6 garlic cloves, finely chopped
2 coriander (cilantro) roots,
   finely chopped
a sprinkle of ground white pepper
20 won ton sheets 7.5 cm
   (3 inches) square
1–2 tablespoons vegetable oil
935 ml (3¾ cups) chicken or vegetable
   stock

2 tablespoons light soy sauce
4 raw prawns (shrimp), peeled
   and deveined
100 g (3½ oz) Chinese cabbage or spinach
   leaves, roughly chopped
100 g (1 cup) bean sprouts, tails removed
3 spring onions (scallions), slivered
ground white pepper, for sprinkling

Serves 4

In a bowl, combine the chopped prawns with 2 of the garlic cloves, the coriander roots, ground pepper and a pinch of salt. Spoon 1 teaspoon of the mixture into the middle of each won ton sheet. Gather up, squeezing the corners together to make a little purse.

Heat the oil in a small wok or frying pan and stir-fry the remaining garlic until light golden. Remove from the heat and discard the garlic.

Heat a saucepan of water to boiling point. Gently drop each won ton purse into the water and cook for 2 to 3 minutes. Lift each won ton out with a slotted spoon and drop it into a bowl of warm water.

Heat the stock in a saucepan to boiling point. Add the light soy sauce, prawns and Chinese cabbage and cook for a few minutes.

Drain the cooked won tons and transfer them to the stock saucepan.

Divide the bean sprouts among individual bowls and divide the won tons and the soup mixture among the bowls. Garnish with spring onions, ground pepper and the garlic oil.

won ton soup with prawns

sesame prawns on toasts

280 g (10 oz) raw prawns (shrimp),
   peeled and deveined
2 teaspoons light soy sauce
1 egg
4–5 large garlic cloves, roughly chopped
7–8 coriander (cilantro) roots, roughly
   chopped
¼ teaspoon ground white pepper
½ teaspoon salt
7 slices day-old white bread, crusts
   removed, each slice cut into two
   triangles
3 tablespoons sesame seeds
peanut oil, for deep-frying
cucumber relish (page 251), to serve

Makes 14

Using a food processor or blender, whiz the prawns into a smooth paste. Transfer to a bowl, add the light soy sauce and egg and mix well. Leave for about 30 minutes to firm.

Using a pestle and mortar, pound the garlic, coriander roots, white pepper and salt into a smooth paste. Add to the prawns. (Using a pestle and mortar gives the best texture but you can also whiz the garlic, coriander roots, pepper, light soy sauce and egg with the prawns.) Heat the grill (broiler) to medium. Spread the bread on a baking tray and put under the grill for 3 to 4 minutes or until the bread is dry and slightly crisp. Spread the prawn paste thickly on one side of each piece. Sprinkle with sesame seeds and press on firmly. Refrigerate for 30 minutes.

Heat the oil in a wok or deep frying pan over a medium heat. Drop in a small cube of bread. If it sizzles immediately, the oil is ready. Deep-fry a few toasts at a time, paste-side down, for 3 minutes or until golden. Turn with a slotted spoon. Drain paste-side up on paper towels. Serve with relish.

หมูแดงราดข้าว

ข้าวผัด

ปู-กุ้ง-หมู-เนื้อ-ไก่ - 20.
ข้าวผัดพริกแกง - 20.
ข้าวผัดกะเพรา - 20.
ข้าวไก่ผัดเม็ดมะม่วง - 20.
ข้าวปูผงกะหรี่ - 20.
ข้าวผัดเปรี้ยวหวาน - 20

5 coriander (cilantro) roots, cleaned
   and roughly chopped
4–5 garlic cloves
1 teaspoon ground white pepper
¼ teaspoon salt
600 g (1 lb 5 oz) skinless chicken breast
   fillets, cut into 25 cubes
2 tablespoons oyster sauce
1½ tablespoons sesame oil
1 tablespoon plain (all-purpose) flour
25 pandanus leaves, cleaned and dried
vegetable oil, for deep-frying
plum sauce or a chilli sauce, to serve

Makes 25

Using a pestle and mortar or a small blender, pound or blend the coriander roots, garlic, white pepper and salt into a paste.

In a bowl, combine the paste with the chicken, oyster sauce, sesame oil and flour. Cover with plastic wrap and marinate in the refrigerator for at least 3 hours, or overnight.

Fold one of the pandanus leaves, bringing the base up in front of the tip, making a cup. Put a piece of chicken in the fold and, moving the bottom of the leaf, wrap it around to create a tie and enclose the chicken. Repeat until you have used all the chicken.

Heat the oil in a wok or deep frying pan over a medium heat.

When the oil seems hot, drop a small piece of leaf into it. If it sizzles immediately, the oil is ready. Lower some parcels into the oil and deep-fry for 7 to 10 minutes or until the parcels feel firm. Lift out with a slotted spoon and drain on paper towels. Keep the cooked ones warm while deep-frying the rest. Transfer to a serving plate. Serve with plum sauce or a chilli sauce.

chicken wrapped
in pandanus leaf

gold bags

280 g (10 oz) raw prawns (shrimp), peeled, deveined and roughly chopped, or skinless chicken or pork fillet, roughly chopped
225 g (8 oz) tin water chestnuts, drained and roughly chopped
3–4 garlic cloves, finely chopped
3 spring onions (scallions), finely sliced
1 tablespoon oyster sauce
1 teaspoon ground white pepper
1 teaspoon salt
2–3 bunches of spring onions (scallions), or 40 chives, for ties
2 tablespoons plain (all-purpose) flour
40 spring roll sheets 13 cm (5 inches) square
peanut oil, for deep-frying
a chilli sauce, to serve

Makes 40

Using a food processor or blender, whiz the prawns, chicken or pork to a fine paste. In a bowl, combine the minced prawn or meat, water chestnuts, garlic, spring onions, oyster sauce, white pepper and salt.

To make spring onion ties, cut each into 4 to 6 strips, using only the longest green parts, then soak them in boiling water for 5 minutes or until soft. Drain, then dry on paper towels.

Mix the flour and 8 tablespoons cold water in a small saucepan until smooth. Stir and cook over a medium heat for 1 to 2 minutes or until thick.

Place 3 spring roll sheets in front of you and keep the remaining sheets in the plastic bag to prevent them drying out. Spoon 2 teaspoons of filling into the middle of each sheet. Brush around the filling with flour paste, then pull up into a bag and pinch together to enclose the filling. Place on a tray that is lightly dusted with flour. Repeat until you have used all the filling and sheets. Tie a piece of spring onion twice around each bag and tie in a knot.

Heat 8 cm (3 inches) oil in a wok or deep frying pan over a medium heat. When the oil seems hot, drop a small piece of spring roll sheet into it. If it sizzles immediately, the oil is ready. It is important not to have the oil too hot or the gold bags will cook too quickly and brown. Lower four bags into the oil and deep-fry for 2 to 3 minutes until they start to go hard. Lower another three or four bags into the oil and deep-fry them all together. To help cook the tops, splash the oil over the tops and deep-fry for 7 to 10 minutes or until golden and crispy. As each batch is cooked, lift the bags out with a slotted spoon and add another batch. Drain on paper towels. Keep the gold bags warm while deep-frying the rest. Serve with a chilli sauce.

350 g (12 oz) raw prawns (shrimp)
1 garlic clove, finely chopped
1 tablespoon coriander (cilantro) leaves,
   finely chopped
½–1 long red chilli, seeded and finely
   chopped
2 teaspoons lime juice
2 teaspoons vegetable oil
1 teaspoon sesame oil
1½ teaspoons light soy sauce
1 tablespoon oyster sauce
¼ teaspoon ground white pepper
4 bamboo sticks

Serves 4

Peel and devein the prawns and cut each prawn along the back so it opens like a butterfly (leave each prawn joined along the base and at the tail).

Put the garlic, coriander, chilli, lime juice, vegetable oil, sesame oil, light soy sauce, oyster sauce and ground pepper in a shallow dish and mix well. Add the prawns to the marinade and mix to coat the prawns. Cover with plastic wrap and marinate in the refrigerator for at least 30 minutes, or overnight.

Soak the bamboo sticks in water for 1 hour to help prevent them from burning during cooking. Thread the prawns onto the sticks.

Heat a barbecue or grill (broiler) to a high heat. If using a grill, line the tray with foil. Grill (broil) the prawns a good distance below the high heat for 8 to 10 minutes on each side. If you cook them directly on a barbecue plate they will cook more quickly, about 4 to 5 minutes. Turn the prawn sticks frequently until the prawns turn pink and are cooked through. You can brush the marinade over the prawns during the cooking. Serve hot.

prawns with coriander leaves and chilli

noodles... Despite the worldwide popularity of *phat Thai* as a main meal, noodle dishes in Thailand are the cheap, fast food sold by street vendors and simple noodle shops. Not considered a basic staple to be shared at the family table like steamed rice, a bowl of noodles is a quick one-stop lunch, a light snack eaten between meetings or a late-night post-party pick-me-up. The stall holders often base their reputation on just one dish.

While the agricultural existence of the country is tied to the cycle of rice growing, noodles are late arrivals, Originally immigrant food cooked up by Chinese vendors on the streets, noodles are still eaten today with chopsticks and a soup spoon, and noodle soups are slurped from big Chinese bowls. However, this does not mean that noodle meals are in any way un-Thai. As they did with other foreign ingredients and techniques, Thai cooks enthusiastically adapted noodles to their own tastes, creating spicy, fresh-tasting noodle dishes quite unlike any others in Asia.

Kuaytiaw are fresh rice noodles and in rice-mad Thailand, unsurprisingly the favourite variety. The fat white ones are those used in *phat Thai*, while the thinnest are deep-fried into tangles to make *mii krob*, crispy sweet and sour noodles, both dishes instantly recognisable as Thai.

Khanom jiin, meaning 'Chinese dessert', are cool, threadlike rice noodles usually served with a coconut curry sauce or spicy relish, a favourite in the south where they sometimes take the place of rice. Among the wheat noodles, Chinese egg noodles, *ba-mii*, are very popular, especially in the north, and *wun sen*, soft, transparent mung bean vermicelli, feature as an ingredient in a few salads and Chinese-style clay-pot dishes and soups.

However vibrantly flavoured, noodles are always served with a selection of condiments for the diner to add as desired. Soy sauce, lime wedges, salt, sugar or chillies, either powdered or cut into a little fish sauce or rice vinegar, are all used to perk up the flavours.

pork sausages

3 coriander (cilantro) roots
1 lemon grass stalk, white part only,
   chopped
4 garlic cloves, chopped
½ teaspoon ground white pepper
1 small red chilli, chopped
2 teaspoons fish sauce
2 teaspoons sugar
300 g (10 oz) minced (ground) pork

Serves 4

Using a pestle and mortar or food processor, pound or blend the coriander, lemon grass, garlic and pepper to a fine paste.

Add the chilli, fish sauce, sugar and pork to the paste mixture and combine well. Form into sausage shapes.

Heat a barbecue or grill (broiler) and cook the sausages for 4 to 5 minutes each side until cooked through.

2 tablespoons peanut oil
4 Asian shallots, finely sliced
2 garlic cloves, smashed with the side
   of a cleaver
150 g (5 oz) minced (ground) chicken
   or pork
2 tablespoons fish sauce
1 tablespoon tamarind purée
1 tablespoon dried shrimp, chopped
2 tablespoons palm sugar
1 cm (½ inch) piece of ginger, grated
2 bird's eye chillies, finely chopped
1 tablespoon roasted peanuts, chopped
1 tablespoon chopped coriander (cilantro)
   leaves
16 betel leaves
lime wedges, for squeezing

Makes 16

Heat the oil in a wok and fry the shallots and garlic for a minute or two until they brown. Add the chicken and fry it until the meat turns opaque, breaking up any lumps with the back of a spoon. Add the fish sauce, tamarind purée, shrimp and palm sugar and cook everything together until the mixture is brown and sticky. Stir in the ginger, chillies, peanuts and coriander leaves.

Lay the betel leaves out on a large plate and top leaf each with some of the mixture. Serve with the lime wedges to squeeze over the mixture.

betel leaves with savoury topping

prawns in a blanket

12 raw large prawns (shrimp), peeled and
   deveined, tails intact
1 tablespoon plain (all-purpose) flour
2 garlic cloves, roughly chopped
3 coriander (cilantro) roots, finely chopped
1 cm (½ inch) piece of ginger, roughly
   sliced
1½ tablespoons oyster sauce or, for a
   hotter flavour, ½ teaspoon red curry
   paste (page 245)

a sprinkle of ground white pepper
12 frozen spring roll sheets or filo sheets,
   12 cm (5 inches) square, defrosted
peanut oil, for deep-frying
a chilli sauce or plum sauce, to serve

Serves 4

To make the prawns easier to wrap, you can make 3 or 4 shallow incisions in the underside of each, then open up the cuts to straighten the prawns.

Mix the flour and 3 tablespoons water in a small saucepan until smooth. Stir and cook over a medium heat for 1 to 2 minutes or until thick. Remove from the heat.

Using a pestle and mortar or a small blender, pound or blend the garlic, coriander roots and ginger together.

In a bowl, combine the garlic paste with the prawns, oyster sauce, pepper and a pinch of salt. Cover with plastic wrap and marinate in the refrigerator for 2 hours, turning occasionally.

Place a spring roll or filo sheet on the work surface and keep all the remaining sheets in the plastic bag to prevent them drying out. Fold the sheet in half, remove a prawn from the marinade and place it on the sheet with its tail sticking out of the top. Fold the bottom up and then the sides in to tightly enclose the prawn. Seal the joins tightly with the flour paste. Repeat with the rest of the prawns and sheets.

Heat the oil in a wok or deep frying pan over a medium heat. When the oil seems hot, drop a small piece of spring roll sheet into it. If it sizzles immediately, the oil is ready. Deep-fry four prawns at a time for 3–4 minutes or until golden brown and crispy. Remove with a slotted spoon and drain on paper towels. Keep the prawns warm while deep-frying the rest. Transfer to a serving plate. Serve hot with chilli sauce or plum sauce.

2 kg (4 lb 8 oz) large mussels in their
    shells (yielding around 350 g/12 oz
    meat)
50 g (2 oz) tapioca or plain (all-purpose)
    flour
40 g (¹/₃ cup) cornflour (cornstarch)
1 tablespoon fish sauce
1 teaspoon sugar
6 garlic cloves, finely chopped
350 g (4 cups) bean sprouts

4 spring onions (scallions), sliced
8 tablespoons vegetable oil
4 large eggs
a few coriander (cilantro) leaves
1 long red chilli, seeded and finely sliced
a sprinkle of ground white pepper
4 lime wedges
a chilli sauce, to serve

Serves 4

Scrub the mussels and remove their hairy beards. Discard any open mussels and any that don't close when tapped on the work surface. Preheat the oven to 180°C/350°F/Gas 4. Spread the mussels over a baking tray and bake for 5 minutes or until the shells open slightly. Discard any unopened mussels. When the shells are cool enough to handle, prise them open, scoop out the meat and put it in a colander to drain out any juices.

Combine the flours with 6 to 8 tablespoons water using a fork or spoon until the mixture is smooth and without lumps. Add the fish sauce and sugar. Divide among four bowls and add some mussels to each bowl.

Separate the garlic, bean sprouts and spring onions into equal portions for each serving.

Make one pancake at a time. Heat 1 tablespoon oil in a small frying pan and stir-fry one portion of garlic over a medium heat until golden brown.

Stir one portion of the mussel mixture with a spoon and pour it into the frying pan, swirling the pan to ensure that the mixture spreads evenly. Cook for 2 to 3 minutes or until it is brown underneath. Turn with a spatula and brown the other side. Make a hole in the centre and break an egg into the hole. Sprinkle a half portion of bean sprouts and spring onion over the top. Cook until the egg sets, then flip the pancake again and turn onto a serving plate. Sprinkle each pancake with coriander leaves, sliced chilli and ground pepper. Place a lime wedge, bean sprouts and spring onions on the plate. Serve with a chilli sauce.

fried mussel pancake

stir-fried white noodles with pork

2 teaspoons oyster sauce
6 teaspoons light soy sauce
1 teaspoon sugar
2 teaspoons yellow bean sauce
1 tablespoon tapioca flour
450 g (1 lb) wide fresh flat rice noodles
  (*sen yai*)
4 tablespoons vegetable oil
4–5 garlic cloves, finely chopped
225 g (8 oz) pork or chicken fillet, finely
  sliced
175 g (6 oz) Chinese kale, cut into 2.5 cm
  (1 inch) pieces, leaves separated
ground white pepper, for sprinkling

SEASONING
6 bird's eye chillies, sliced and mixed
  with 3 tablespoons white vinegar
3 tablespoons fish sauce
3 tablespoons roasted chilli powder
3 tablespoons white sugar

Serves 4

Mix the oyster sauce, 4 teaspoons of the light soy sauce, sugar, yellow bean sauce and tapioca flour with 125 ml (½ cup) water in a bowl.

Put the noodles in a bowl with 2 teaspoons of the soy sauce and rub the sauce through the noodles, separating them out as you do so.

Heat 2 tablespoons oil in a wok or frying pan over a medium heat and stir-fry the noodles for 4 to 5 minutes or until the noodles are browning at the edges and beginning to stick. Keep them warm on a serving plate.

Heat the remaining oil in a wok or frying pan and stir-fry the garlic over a medium heat until light brown. Add the pork and stir-fry for 2 to 3 minutes or until the meat is cooked. Add the stalks of Chinese kale and stir-fry for 1 to 2 minutes. Add the sauce mixture and the top leaves and stir together for another minute or so. Taste and adjust the seasoning if necessary.

Spoon the pork and Chinese kale on top of the noodles and sprinkle with white pepper. Serve the seasoning ingredients in small bowls on the side, for adjusting the flavour.

50 g (2 oz) vermicelli, cellophane or wun
   sen noodles
15 g (½ oz) dried black fungus (about half
   a handful)
2 tablespoons plain (all-purpose) flour
1½ tablespoons vegetable oil
3–4 garlic cloves, finely chopped
100 g (3½ oz) minced (ground) chicken
   or pork
1 small carrot, finely grated
140 g (1⅔ cups) bean sprouts

1 cm (½ inch) piece of ginger,
   finely grated
1½–2 tablespoons fish sauce
1½ tablespoons oyster sauce
¼ teaspoon ground white pepper
25 spring roll sheets 13 cm (5 inches)
   square
peanut oil, for deep-frying
a chilli sauce, to serve

Makes 25 small spring rolls

Soak the vermicelli in hot water for 1 to 2 minutes or until soft. Drain, then cut into small pieces. Soak the dried mushrooms in hot water for 2 to 3 minutes or until soft. Drain, then finely chop. To make a paste, stir the flour and 2 tablespoons of water together in a small bowl until smooth.

Heat the oil in a wok or frying pan and stir-fry the garlic until golden brown. Add the chicken or pork and using a spoon, break the meat until it separates into small bits and is cooked. Add the vermicelli, mushrooms, carrot, bean sprouts, ginger, fish sauce, oyster sauce and white pepper. Cook for another 4 to 5 minutes. Taste, then adjust the seasoning. Allow to cool.

Place 3 spring roll sheets on a work surface and spread some flour paste around the edges. Keep the remaining sheets in the plastic bag. Spoon 2 teaspoons of filling onto a sheet along the side nearest to you, about 2.5 cm (1 inch) from the edge. Bring the edge up, then roll it away from you a half turn over the filling. Fold the sides into the centre to enclose the filling, then wrap and seal the join tightly with the flour paste. Repeat with the rest of the filling and wrappers.

Heat 5 cm (2 inches) oil in a wok or deep frying pan over a medium heat. When the oil seems hot, drop a small piece of spring roll sheet into the oil. If it sizzles immediately, the oil is ready. Don't have the oil too hot. Lower five rolls into the oil and deep-fry for 2 to 3 minutes. When they start to go hard, lower another four rolls into the oil and deep-fry them all together. To help cook the tops, splash oil over the tops. Deep-fry for 6 to 8 minutes or until crispy. As the spring rolls cook, lift out one at a time with a slotted spoon and add another. Drain on paper towels. Serve with a chilli sauce.

spring rolls

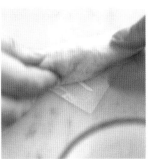

phat thai

150 g (5 oz) dried noodles (*sen lek*)
300 g (10 oz) raw large prawns (shrimp)
3 tablespoons tamarind purée
2½ tablespoons fish sauce
2 tablespoons palm sugar
3 tablespoons vegetable oil
3–4 garlic cloves, finely chopped
2 eggs
85 g (3 oz) Chinese chives (1 bunch)
¼ teaspoon chilli powder, depending on taste
2 tablespoons dried shrimp, ground or pounded

2 tablespoons preserved turnip, finely chopped
2½–3 tablespoons chopped roasted peanuts
180 g (2 cups) bean sprouts
3 spring onions (scallions), slivered
1 long red chilli, seeded and shredded, for garnish
a few coriander (cilantro) leaves, for garnish
lime wedges, to serve

Serves 4

Soak the noodles in hot water for 1 to 2 minutes or until soft, then drain.

Peel and devein the prawns and cut each prawn along the back so it opens like a butterfly (leave each prawn joined along the base and at the tail, leaving the tail attached).

Combine the tamarind with the fish sauce and palm sugar in a bowl.

Heat 1½ tablespoons oil in a wok or frying pan and stir-fry the garlic over a medium heat until light brown. Add the prawns and cook for 2 minutes.

Using a spatula, move the prawns out from the middle of the wok. Add another 1½ tablespoons oil to the wok. Add the eggs and stir to scramble for 1 minute. Add the noodles and chives and stir-fry for a few seconds. Add the fish sauce mixture, chilli powder, dried shrimp, preserved turnip and half of the peanuts. Add half of the bean sprouts and spring onions. Test the noodles for tenderness and adjust the seasoning if necessary.

Spoon onto the serving plate and sprinkle the remaining peanuts over the top. Garnish with shredded chillies and a few coriander leaves. Place the lime wedges and remaining bean sprouts and spring onions at the side of the dish and serve.

***phrik* (chillies)...** Thai food is renowned as one of the hottest cuisines, its use of chillies legendary and its fiery dishes feared by the uninitiated. Indeed, it is hard to believe that chillies are not indigenous to the country and the cooking. In fact, they were brought to Thailand by the Portuguese in the seventeenth century and until as late as the twentieth century, Thai dishes were much more subtly seasoned, spiced predominantly with peppercorns.

Chillies are used in Thai cooking not just for heat but for flavour, aroma and colour, the last unusually important to presentation-conscious Thai cooks, who will tuck bright-red chillies into green salads and crush red, yellow and green chillies to give rich colour to their curry pastes.

A dozen chilli varieties thrive today in Thailand and different ones are matched to different dishes. The much-loved and tiny bird's eye or 'mouse droppings' chillies are the variety that has given Thai food its red-hot reputation. Usually green, though sometimes red, if you can get past their sting they have a wonderful floral flavour that makes them hard to substitute. They are often added whole to salads, relishes and curries because simply cutting them up can make them hotter.

Long, or sky-pointing, red, green or yellow chillies are milder and are used in salads, stir-fries and curries, especially in the less scorching cooking of central and northern Thailand.

Dried chillies are also used to give a more mellow taste to dishes. While dishes containing fresh green chillies tend to be cooked for a shorter time to keep flavours fresh, red curries made with dried long red chillies are cooked a little longer to give a nutty, spicy taste and fragrance.

And if your meal is just not spicy enough, powdered and sliced chillies are always provided as condiments to add a little verve as required.

1½ tablespoons vegetable oil
2–3 garlic cloves, finely chopped
225 g (8 oz) minced (ground) pork
1 spring onion (scallion), finely sliced
½ tablespoon coriander (cilantro) leaves,
   finely chopped
25 g (1 oz) unsalted cooked peanuts,
   roughly ground
2 tablespoons light soy sauce
3 tablespoons palm sugar
a pinch of ground white pepper
16 small segments of pineapple, or
   tangerine, mandarin or orange segments
a few coriander (cilantro) leaves, for
   garnish
1 red chilli, very finely sliced, for garnish

Serves 4

Heat the oil in a saucepan or wok and stir-fry the garlic until golden brown.
Add the pork and cook over a medium heat. With a spoon, break up the
meat until it has separated and is almost dry. Add the spring onion, coriander
leaves, ground peanuts, light soy sauce, sugar and pepper. Stir together for
4 to 5 minutes or until the mixture is dry and sticky.

If you are using pineapple, spoon some mixture onto each segment.

If using citrus fruit, cut each segment from top to bottom, around the outer
curve, and open each up like a butterfly. Remove any pips.

Arrange the segments on a serving plate and, with a teaspoon, transfer a
little pork mixture onto each piece. Place a coriander leaf and a slice of chilli
on top of each.

galloping horses

pork on sticks

1 kg (2 lb 4 oz) fillet of pork
250 ml (1 cup) coconut milk
2 tablespoons coconut sugar
2 tablespoons light soy sauce
2 tablespoons oyster sauce
110 g (4 oz) Asian shallots, roughly
   chopped
4 garlic cloves, roughly chopped
5 coriander (cilantro) roots, finely chopped
2.5 cm (1 inch) piece of ginger, sliced
1½ teaspoons ground turmeric
¼ teaspoon ground white pepper
25 bamboo skewers, 18–20 cm
   (7–8 inches) long

Makes 25

Cut the pork into pieces 4 cm (1½ inches) wide x 8 cm (3 inches) long x 5 mm (¼ inch) thick and put them in a bowl.

Mix the coconut milk, sugar, light soy sauce, oyster sauce, shallots, garlic, coriander roots, ginger, turmeric and white pepper in a bowl until the sugar has dissolved. Pour over the meat and mix using your fingers or a spoon. Cover with plastic wrap and refrigerate for at least 5 hours, or overnight, turning occasionally.

Soak the bamboo skewers in water for 1 hour to help prevent them from burning during cooking.

Thread a piece of the marinated pork onto each skewer as if you were sewing a piece of material. If some pieces are small, thread two pieces onto each skewer. Heat a barbecue or grill (broiler) to high heat. If using a grill, line the grill tray with foil.

Barbecue for 5 to 7 minutes on each side, or grill (broil) the pork for 10 minutes on each side, until cooked through and slightly charred. Turn frequently and brush the marinade over the meat during the cooking. If using the grill, cook a good distance below the heat. Serve hot or warm.

110 g (4 oz) minced (ground) raw prawns
  (shrimp)
80 g (½ cup) water chestnuts, drained and
  roughly chopped
1 garlic clove, finely chopped
1 spring onion (scallion), finely chopped
1 tablespoon oyster sauce
¼ teaspoon salt
¼ teaspoon pepper
30–35 won ton sheets 7.5 cm (3 inches)
  square
peanut oil, for deep-frying
sweet chilli sauce or other chilli sauce,
  to serve

Makes about 30

Combine the prawns with the water chestnuts, garlic and spring onion in a
bowl. Mix in the oyster sauce, salt and pepper. Spoon about ½ teaspoon
of mixture into the middle of each won ton sheet. Gather up, squeezing the
corners together to make a little purse. Place on a tray. Continue until you
have used up all the sheets and filling.

Heat 5 cm (2 inches) oil in a wok or deep frying pan over a medium heat.
When the oil seems hot, drop a small piece of won ton sheet into the oil.
If it sizzles immediately, the oil is ready. Don't have the oil too hot or the
purses will burn.

Lower five purses into the oil. After 2 to 3 minutes they will start to go hard.
Lower another four to five purses into the oil and deep-fry them all together.
To help cook the tops, spoon some of the oil over the tops. Deep-fry for
another 3 to 4 minutes or until golden brown and crispy. As each batch
cooks, lift out the purses with a slotted spoon and add some more in their
place. Drain on paper towels. Keep warm while deep-frying the remaining
purses. Transfer to a serving plate. Serve with chilli sauce.

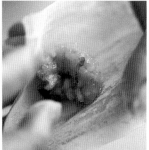

gold purses

a little taste of...

The contribution of the royal court to the cooking of Thailand is perhaps more significant than in any other nation. Of course, the best cuisine is always going to be centred around a wealthy aristocracy, but Thai royalty, by using food as a status symbol to set themselves apart from their agricultural society, elevated the art of cooking to high culture and encouraged immense creativity among Thai chefs. It was thus the aristocracy who mainly recorded Thai recipes, with even kings penning their own cookbooks.

Royal cuisine has, despite this, always been surprisingly similar to the food eaten by the majority of the population, the biggest difference being the high quality of produce and exquisite presentation. Elegant, subtle and refined, this Thai *haute cuisine* tends to be served as part of a multi-course affair, the emphasis on smaller portions and beautiful fruit and vegetable carving, an artform passed down from the Court to even the humblest fruit-sellers. Today, with the royal recipes now open to all, the highest expression of Thai cooking is maintained and evolves not in the palace, but in the country's finest restaurants.

...the
...luc kitchn

tom yam kung

350 g (12 oz) raw prawns (shrimp)
1 tablespoon oil
3 lemon grass stalks, white part only,
   bruised
3 thin slices of galangal
2 litres (8 cups) chicken stock or water
5–7 bird's eye chillies, stems removed,
   bruised
5 makrut (kaffir) lime leaves, torn
2 tablespoons fish sauce
70 g (2 oz) straw mushrooms, or
   quartered button mushrooms
2 spring onions (scallions), sliced
3 tablespoons lime juice
a few coriander (cilantro) leaves,
   for garnish

Serves 4

Peel and devein the prawns, leaving the tails intact and reserving the heads and shells. Heat the oil in a large stockpot or wok and add the prawn heads and shells. Cook for 5 minutes or until the shells turn bright orange.

Add one stalk of lemon grass to the pan with the galangal and stock or water. Bring to the boil, then reduce the heat and simmer for 20 minutes. Strain the stock and return to the pan. Discard the shells and flavourings.

Finely slice the remaining lemon grass and add it to the liquid with the chillies, lime leaves, fish sauce, mushrooms and spring onions. Cook gently for 2 minutes.

Add the prawns and cook for 3 minutes or until the prawns are firm and pink. Take off the heat and add the lime juice. Taste, then adjust the seasoning with extra lime juice or fish sauce if necessary. Garnish with coriander leaves.

1 large pomelo
1 tablespoon fish sauce
1 tablespoon lime juice
1 teaspoon sugar
1 tablespoon chilli jam (page 250)
300 g (10 oz) raw medium prawns
   (shrimp), peeled and deveined,
   tails intact
3 tablespoons shredded fresh coconut,
   lightly toasted until golden (if fresh is
   unavailable, use shredded or desiccated)
3 Asian shallots, finely sliced
5 bird's eye chillies, bruised
20 g (1 cup) mint leaves
10 g (1/3 cup) coriander (cilantro) leaves
1 tablespoon fried Asian shallots

Serves 4

To peel a pomelo, first, slice a circular patch off the top of the fruit, about 2 cm (3/4 inch) deep (roughly the thickness of the skin). Next, score four deep lines from top to bottom, dividing the skin into four segments. Peel away the skin, one quarter at a time. Remove any remaining pith and separate the segments of the fruit. Peel the segments and remove any seeds. Crumble the segments into their component parts, without squashing them or releasing any of the juice.

To make the dressing, combine the fish sauce, lime juice, sugar and chilli jam in a small bowl and stir.

Bring a large saucepan of water to the boil. Add the prawns and cook for 2 minutes. Drain and allow the prawns to cool.

In a large bowl, gently combine the pomelo, prawns, toasted coconut, shallots, chillies, mint and coriander. Just before serving, add the dressing and toss gently to combine all the ingredients. Sprinkle with fried shallots and serve.

prawn and pomelo salad

curried fish steamed in banana chillies

FISH FILLING
4–5 dried long red chillies
3 garlic cloves, roughly chopped
1–2 Asian shallots, roughly chopped
4 coriander (cilantro) roots, roughly chopped
1 lemon grass stalk, white part only, finely sliced
1 cm (½ inch) piece of galangal, finely chopped
2 makrut (kaffir) lime leaves, finely sliced
1 teaspoon shrimp paste
275 g (10 oz) firm white fish fillets, cut into 1 cm (½ inch) pieces, or small raw prawns (shrimp) or small scallops

410 ml (1⅔ cups) coconut milk
2 eggs
2 tablespoons fish sauce

10 banana chillies, or small capsicums (peppers), preferably elongated ones
2 handfuls of Thai sweet basil leaves
2 tablespoons coconut cream
3–4 makrut (kaffir) lime leaves, finely sliced, for garnish
1 long red chilli, seeded, finely sliced, for garnish

Serves 4

To make the fish filling, using a pestle and mortar or blender, pound or blend the chillies, garlic, shallots and coriander roots together. Add the lemon grass, galangal, makrut lime leaves, shrimp paste and ¼ teaspoon salt, one ingredient at a time, until the mixture forms a curry paste. In a bowl, combine the curry paste, fish, coconut milk, eggs and fish sauce. Keep stirring in the same direction for 10 minutes, then cover and refrigerate for 30 minutes to set slightly.

If using chillies, or if the capsicums are the long ones, make a long cut with a sharp knife; or if they are the round ones, cut a small round slice from the tops. Remove the seeds and membrane, then clean the chillies or capsicums and pat them dry. Place a few basil leaves in the bottom of each. Spoon in the fish mixture until it nearly reaches the top edge.

Fill a wok or a steamer pan with water, cover and bring to a rolling boil over a high heat. Place the chillies or capsicums on a plate. Use a plate that will fit on the rack of a traditional bamboo steamer basket or on a steamer rack inside the wok or pan. Set the basket or rack over the water and put the plate on the rack. Reduce the heat to a simmer. Cover and cook for 15 to 20 minutes. Check and replenish the water after 10 minutes.

Turn off the heat and transfer the chillies or capsicums to a serving plate. Spoon the coconut cream on top and sprinkle with lime leaves and chilli.

2 tablespoons fish sauce
2 tablespoons lime juice
2 teaspoons palm sugar
2 green bird's eye chillies, chopped
2 red bird's eye chillies, chopped
1 teaspoon ground dried shrimp
300 g (10 oz) fresh crab meat
30 g (²/₃ cup) chopped mint leaves
20 g (¹/₃ cup) chopped coriander (cilantro)
leaves
4 Asian shallots, finely sliced
1 green mango, flesh finely shredded
1 tomato, cut in half lengthways and
thinly sliced
1 large green chilli, thinly sliced on
an angle

Serves 4

To make a dressing, put the fish sauce, lime juice, palm sugar, bird's eye chillies and dried shrimp in a small bowl and stir to dissolve the sugar.

Just before serving, put the crab meat, mint and coriander leaves, shallots, mango and tomato in a large bowl and toss gently.

Pour the dressing over the salad, then toss to combine and serve with the sliced chilli on top.

crab and green mango salad

prawns with thai sweet basil leaves

600 g (1 lb 5 oz) raw prawns (shrimp)
2 tablespoons vegetable oil
2 tablespoons dry curry paste (page 248)
    or bought paste
185 ml (¾ cup) coconut milk
2 teaspoons fish sauce
2 teaspoons palm sugar
a handful of Thai sweet basil leaves,
    for garnish
1 long red chilli, seeded and finely sliced,
    for garnish

Serves 4

Peel and devein the prawns and cut each prawn along the back so it opens like a butterfly (leave each prawn joined along the base and at the tail, leaving the tail attached).

Heat the oil in a saucepan or wok and stir-fry the dry curry paste over a medium heat for 2 minutes or until fragrant.

Add the coconut milk, fish sauce and palm sugar and cook for a few seconds. Add the prawns and cook for a few minutes or until the prawns are cooked through. Taste, then adjust the seasoning if necessary. Spoon into a serving bowl and garnish with basil leaves and chillies.

tom (soups)

Thai soups are not quite what you might expect from the name. A unique component of most meals, they are neither the individual bowls of chicken noodle or minestrone soup found in western cooking nor the digestive broths of Chinese and Japanese cuisine. Instead, a *tom* is brought to the table with all the other dishes, another jigsaw piece in the ideal of a harmonious, balanced meal. Ladled into small bowls, the occasional spoonful is sipped during a dinner to counterbalance other flavours. Thought of only as part of the whole, never as a dish that stands alone, Thai soups can vary enormously, some bursting with spicy, strong flavours, others almost delicate, balancing the sharp tastes or cutting the richness of other dishes.

To many outside the country, *tom yam* is one of the best known of Thailand's dishes, a hot prawn soup aromatic with lemon grass and makrut (kaffir) lime

leaves. In fact, this soup is properly called *tom yam kung* and to the Thais *tom*, which literally means 'to boil' and yam, to 'mix', indicate any in a range of hot and sour soups. A *tom yam*, with its intense combination of heat, astringency and a sweet fragrance, is a liquid version of the most essential elements of Thai cooking and is usually made from a paste in the same way as a simple curry.

Similarly, *tom khaa* is not the name for Thai chicken soup, but means 'boiled galangal' and can point to any of a number of gentler, sweeter versions of *tom yam*, made from lots of galangal and split coconut milk. *Kaeng jut* translates as the unpretentious 'bland soup', and these warming broths appear to have originated in China. The occasional spoonful during the meal not only helps to take the heat out of spicy dishes, it also revives the palate in readiness for the next chilli attack.

750 ml (3 cups) coconut milk
2 lemon grass stalks, white part only,
  each cut into a tassel or bruised
5 cm (2 inch) piece of galangal, cut into
  several pieces
4 Asian shallots, smashed with the flat
  side of a cleaver
400 g (14 oz) skinless chicken breast
  fillets, cut into slices
2 tablespoons fish sauce
1 tablespoon palm sugar
200 g (7 oz) baby tomatoes, cut into
  bite-sized pieces if large

150 g (5 oz) straw mushrooms or button
  mushrooms
3 tablespoons lime juice
6 makrut (kaffir) lime leaves, torn in half
3–5 bird's eye chillies, stems removed,
  bruised, or 2 long red chillies, seeded
  and finely sliced
a few coriander (cilantro) leaves, for
  garnish

Serves 4

Put the coconut milk, lemon grass, galangal and shallots in a saucepan or wok over a medium heat and bring to a boil.

Add the chicken, fish sauce and palm sugar and simmer, stirring constantly for 5 minutes or until the chicken is cooked through.

Add the tomatoes and mushrooms and simmer for 2 to 3 minutes. Add the lime juice, makrut lime leaves and chillies in the last few seconds, taking care not to let the tomatoes lose their shape. Taste, then adjust the seasoning if necessary. This dish is not meant to be overwhelmingly hot, but to have a sweet, salty, sour taste. Serve garnished with coriander leaves.

tom khaa kai

laap pet

1 tablespoon jasmine rice
280 g (10 oz) minced (ground) duck
3 tablespoons lime juice
1 tablespoon fish sauce
2 lemon grass stalks, white part only,
    finely sliced
50 g (2 oz) Asian shallots, finely sliced
5 makrut (kaffir) lime leaves, finely sliced
5 spring onions (scallions), finely chopped
¼–½ teaspoon roasted chilli powder,
    according to taste
a few lettuce leaves
a few mint leaves, for garnish
raw vegetables such as snake beans,
    cut into lengths, cucumber slices,
    thin wedges of cabbage, halved baby
    tomatoes, to serve

Serves 4

Dry-fry the rice in a small pan over a medium heat. Shake the pan to move the rice around for 6 to 8 minutes, or until the rice is brown. Using a pestle and mortar or a small blender, pound or blend the rice until it almost forms a powder.

In a saucepan or wok, cook the duck with the lime juice and fish sauce over a high heat. Crumble and break the duck until the meat has separated into small pieces. Cook until light brown. Dry, then remove from the heat.

Add the rice powder, lemon grass, shallots, makrut lime leaves, spring onions and chilli powder to the duck pieces and stir together. Taste, then adjust the seasoning if necessary.

Line a serving plate with lettuce leaves. Spoon the duck over the leaves, then garnish with mint leaves. Arrange the vegetables on a separate plate.

75 g (3 oz) rice vermicelli noodles
vegetable oil, for deep-frying
200 g (7 oz) firm tofu (bean curd), cut into
    matchsticks
75 g (3 oz) small Asian shallots or small
    red onions, finely sliced
150 g (5 oz) raw prawns (shrimp), peeled
    and deveined, tails intact
2 tablespoons fish sauce
2 tablespoons water or pickled garlic juice
1 tablespoon lime juice
2 tablespoons plum sauce or tomato
    ketchup

1 tablespoon sweet chilli sauce
4 tablespoons sugar
3 tablespoons palm sugar
3 small whole pickled garlic, finely sliced
110 g (1¼ cups) bean sprouts, tails
    removed, for garnish
3–4 spring onions (scallions), slivered,
    for garnish
1 long red chilli, seeded and cut into
    slivers, for garnish

Serves 4

Soak the noodles in cold water for 20 minutes, drain and dry very thoroughly on paper towels. Cut them into smaller lengths with a pair of scissors.

Put the oil in the wok to a depth of about 8 to 10 cm (3 to 4 inches) and heat over a medium heat. Drop a piece of noodle into the wok. If it sinks and then immediately floats and puffs, the oil is ready. Drop a small handful of the noodles into the oil. Turn them once (it only takes seconds) and remove them as soon as they have swelled and turned a dark ivory colour. Remove the crispy noodles with a slotted spoon, briefly hold over the wok to drain, then transfer to a baking tray lined with paper towels to drain. Fry the remaining noodles in the same way. Break into smaller bits.

In the same oil, deep-fry the tofu for 7 to 10 minutes or until golden and crisp. Remove and drain with a slotted spoon. Deep-fry the shallots until crispy and golden brown. Remove with a slotted spoon and drain on paper towels. Deep-fry the prawns for 1 to 2 minutes until they turn pink. Remove with a slotted spoon and drain on paper towels.

Carefully pour off all the oil in the wok. Add the fish sauce, water, lime juice, plum sauce, sweet chilli sauce, sugar and palm sugar to the wok. Stir for 4 to 5 minutes over a low heat until slightly thickened. Add half of the rice noodles and toss gently, mixing them into the sauce. Add the remaining noodles and the tofu, prawns, pickled garlic and the shallots, tossing for 1 to 2 minutes until coated. Spoon onto a platter and garnish with bean sprouts, spring onions and chilli slivers.

mii krob

red curry with roasted duck and lychees

60 ml (¼ cup) coconut cream
2 tablespoons red curry paste (page 245)
   or bought paste
½ roasted duck, boned and chopped
440 ml (1¾ cups) coconut milk
2 tablespoons fish sauce
1 tablespoon palm sugar
225 g (8 oz) tin lychees, drained
110 g (4 oz) baby tomatoes
7 makrut (kaffir) lime leaves, torn in half
a handful of Thai sweet basil leaves,
   for garnish
1 long red chilli, seeded and finely sliced,
   for garnish

Serves 4

Put the coconut cream in a wok or saucepan and simmer over a medium heat for about 5 minutes, or until the cream separates and a layer of oil forms on the surface. Stir the cream if it starts to brown around the edges. Add the curry paste, stir well to combine and cook until fragrant.

Add the roasted duck and stir for 5 minutes. Add the coconut milk, fish sauce and palm sugar and simmer over a medium heat for another 5 minutes. Add the lychees and baby tomatoes and cook for 1 to 2 minutes. Add the makrut lime leaves. Taste, then adjust the seasoning if necessary. Spoon into a serving bowl and sprinkle with the basil leaves and sliced chilli.

yam (salads)

In many Asian countries, little raw food is eaten apart from peeled fruit, but in Thailand salads are a major feature of the cuisine. The piquant, startling flavours of these *yam* may be unfamiliar to westerners used to green salads and coleslaw, but the combination of vegetables, flowers, chilled seafood or meat tossed in a sour and often extremely hot relish is unmistakeably Thai and, once sampled, an obvious treatment for the freshest of raw ingredients.

There are hundreds of possible *yam* combinations, *yam* meaning literally to 'mix together', but the key, as with much of Thai cooking, is in the balance of sour, sweet, salty and spicy flavours, both among the main ingredients and in the dressing.

The fact that these are chilled, mainly uncooked dishes makes the flavours even more intense, and a *yam* can be very unforgiving to prepare. The finest produce is essential to create its fresh burst of flavour. Among the ingredients, fruit often provides the sweet, tart tastes: pomelo, unripe mango and the sour green papaya used in the classic north-eastern salad, *som tam* are all favourites.

Yams are as much about texture as taste, so differently textured ingredients are added to temper the sour fruit. Chopping and cutting techniques are paramount to bringing the most out of the fresh ingredients. Vegetables can be raw or lightly cooked, but they always maintain a crispy texture; while crunchy, crumbled fish; silky, poached chicken; or the spicy minced meat in *laap*, the salad of the north-east, are all variations. Roasted coconut, peanuts and whole chillies add salty and spicy shades to the dish.

Such strong ingredients are needed to stand up to the tangy dressings: hot combinations of sour lime, sweet palm sugar, spicy chilli and salty fish sauce. Even the salad garnishes are part of the ensemble: brightly coloured chilli slices and shallots scattered over with handfuls of aromatic herbs. The serving of *yams* does not conform to any rules. They can be dished up with other courses or nibbled on before a meal. They are also eaten more like a snack or even over rice in the same way as a curry, especially the northern charcoal-grilled beef salads, devoured with sticky rice and chilled beer.

3 tablespoons lime juice
1 large banana blossom
250 ml (1 cup) coconut cream
200 g (7 oz) skinless chicken breast fillet,
    trimmed
1 tablespoon chilli jam (page 250)
1 tablespoon fish sauce
1 tablespoon palm sugar
2 teaspoons lime juice
12 cherry tomatoes, cut in halves
20 g (1 cup) mint leaves
10 g (⅓ cup) coriander (cilantro) leaves
1 makrut (kaffir) lime leaf, finely
    shredded, for garnish

Serves 4

Put the lime juice in a large bowl of cold water. Using a stainless-steel knife, remove the outer leaves of the banana blossom until you reach the creamy pale centre. Cut the heart or centre into quarters and remove the hard cores and stamens from each. Finely slice the fleshy heart on an angle and place the slices in the lime water until ready to use.

Reserve 2 tablespoons of the coconut cream and pour the rest into a small saucepan and bring to a boil. Add the chicken breast, return to a boil, then reduce the heat and simmer for 5 minutes. Remove from the heat and cover the pan with a tight lid for 20 minutes. Remove the chicken from the pan and discard the cream. When cool, shred the chicken into bite-sized pieces.

In a small bowl, combine the reserved coconut cream with the chilli jam, fish sauce, palm sugar and lime juice.

Just before serving, drain the banana blossom and put it in a large bowl or plate with the shredded chicken, tomato halves, and mint and coriander leaves. Add the dressing and gently toss to combine the ingredients. Garnish with the shredded makrut lime leaf.

shredded chicken and banana blossom

fried rice with pineapple

1 fresh pineapple, leaves attached
2 tablespoons vegetable oil
1 egg, beaten with a pinch of salt
2–3 garlic cloves, finely chopped
150 g (5 oz) raw prawns (shrimp),
    peeled and deveined
150 g (5 oz) ham, finely chopped
25 g (1 oz) sweet corn kernels
25 g (1 oz) peas
½ red capsicum (pepper), finely diced
1 tablespoon finely sliced ginger (optional)

280 g (1½ cups) cooked jasmine rice,
    refrigerated overnight
1 tablespoon light soy sauce
25 g (1 oz) roasted salted cashew nuts,
    roughly chopped
1 long red chilli, seeded and finely sliced,
    for garnish
a few coriander (cilantro) leaves, for
    garnish

Serves 4

Preheat the oven to 180°C/350°F/Gas 4. Cut the pineapple in half, lengthways. Scoop the flesh out of both halves using a tablespoon and a paring knife, to leave two shells with a 1 cm (½ inch) border of flesh attached. Cut the pineapple flesh into small cubes. Put half the cubes in a bowl and refrigerate the rest for eating later.

Wrap the pineapple leaves in foil to prevent them from burning. Place the shells on a baking tray and bake for 10 to 15 minutes. This will seal in the juice and prevent it leaking into the fried rice when it is placed in the shells.

Heat 1 tablespoon oil in a wok or frying pan over a medium heat. Pour in the egg and swirl the pan so that the egg coats it, forming a thin omelette. Cook for 2 minutes, or until the egg is set and slightly brown on the underside, then flip over to brown the other side. Remove from the pan and allow to cool slightly. Roll up and cut into thin strips.

Heat 1 tablespoon oil in the wok or frying pan and stir-fry the garlic over a medium heat until light brown. Add the prawns, ham, sweet corn, peas, capsicum and ginger. Stir-fry for 2 minutes or until the prawns open and turn pink. Add the cooked rice, light soy sauce and the bowl of fresh pineapple and toss together over a medium heat for 5 to 7 minutes. Taste, then adjust the seasoning if necessary.

Spoon as much of the fried rice as will fit into the pineapple shells and sprinkle with cashew nuts and omelette strips. Garnish with sliced chillies and coriander leaves.

a little taste of...

A visit to bustling, contemporary Bangkok can make Thailand appear very urban, but in many ways the country remains predominantly an agricultural society. The food most people eat everyday therefore reflects the simple, labour-intensive lifestyle of the paddy fields. Many families cook in an outside kitchen; the simplest meal is rice, grilled fish and *naam phrik*, chilli relish, everything prepared quickly to fit around the work of the land.

The central plains of Thailand are dominated by paddy fields, and the fertile land of the country's heart allows many families there to be essentially self-sustaining. Even a small farm can provide rice, vegetables, a few wild herbs, fruit from the orchards, fish dredged from the *klongs*, canals, and frogs and insects caught literally in the paddies. With such a wealth of ingredients, there is little need to hunt, the diet only occasionally supplemented by a little meat or chicken. Even in the hills of the northeast or along the hot southern coastline, the Thais can pick corn and sticky rice, or gather coconuts, pineapples and fish.

...the
paddy fields

110 g (4 oz) raw prawns (shrimp)
2 tablespoons vegetable oil
3–4 large garlic cloves, finely chopped
1 coriander (cilantro) root, finely chopped
1 garlic clove, extra, roughly chopped
a pinch of ground white pepper, plus extra,
   to sprinkle
75 g (3 oz) minced (ground) chicken or
   pork
1 spring onion (scallion), finely chopped
935 ml (3¾ cups) chicken or vegetable
   stock

2 tablespoons light soy sauce
2 teaspoons preserved radish
325 g (1¾ cups) cooked jasmine rice
1 tablespoon finely sliced ginger
1 Chinese cabbage leaf, roughly chopped
2 spring onions (scallions), finely chopped,
   for garnish
a few coriander (cilantro) leaves, for
   garnish

Serves 4

Peel and devein the prawns and cut each prawn along the back so it opens like a butterfly (leave each prawn joined along the base and at the tail, leaving the tail attached).

Heat the oil in a small wok or frying pan and stir-fry the finely chopped garlic until light golden. Remove from the heat and discard the garlic.

Using a pestle and mortar or a small blender, pound or blend the coriander root, roughly chopped garlic, pepper and a pinch of salt into a paste. In a bowl, combine the coriander paste with the chicken or pork and spring onion. Using a spoon or your wet hands, shape the mixture into small balls about 1 cm (½ inch) across.

Heat the stock to boiling point in a saucepan. Add the light soy sauce, preserved radish and rice. Lower the meatballs into the stock over a medium heat and cook for 3 minutes or until the chicken is cooked. Add the prawns, ginger and Chinese cabbage to the stock. Cook for another 1 to 2 minutes or until the prawns open and turn pink. Taste, then adjust the seasoning if necessary.

Garnish with spring onions and coriander leaves. Sprinkle with ground white pepper and the garlic oil.

rice soup with prawns and chicken

pork with
sweet and sour sauce

225 g (8 oz) tin pineapple slices in
  light syrup, each slice cut into
  4 pieces (reserve the syrup)
1½ tablespoons plum sauce or
  tomato ketchup
2½ teaspoons fish sauce
1 tablespoon sugar
2 tablespoons vegetable oil
250 g (9 oz) pork, sliced
4 garlic cloves, finely chopped
¼ carrot, sliced
1 medium onion, cut into 8 slices

½ red capsicum (pepper), cut into
  bite-sized pieces
1 small cucumber, unpeeled, halved
  lengthways and cut into thick slices
1 tomato, cut into 4 slices, or 4–5 baby
  tomatoes
a few coriander (cilantro) leaves, for
  garnish

Serves 4

Mix all the pineapple syrup (about 6 tablespoons) with the plum sauce, fish sauce and sugar in a small bowl until smooth.

Heat the oil in a wok or deep frying pan over a medium heat and fry the pork until nicely browned and cooked. Lift out with a slotted spoon and drain on paper towels.

Add the garlic to the wok or pan and fry over a medium heat for 1 minute or until lightly browned. Add the carrot, onion and capsicum and stir-fry for 1 to 2 minutes. Add the cucumber, tomato, pineapple and pineapple syrup and stir together for another minute. Taste, then adjust the seasoning if necessary.

Return the pork to the pan and gently stir. Spoon onto a serving plate and garnish with coriander leaves.

1–2 dried long red chillies
1 tablespoon fish sauce
2 tablespoons oyster sauce
3 tablespoons chicken or vegetable
   stock, or water
½–1 teaspoon sugar
4 tablespoons vegetable oil
80 g (½ cup) cashew nuts
4–5 garlic cloves, finely chopped
500 g (1 lb 2 oz) skinless chicken
   breast fillets, finely sliced

½ red capsicum (pepper), cut into
   thin strips
½ carrot, sliced diagonally
1 small onion, cut into 6 wedges
2 spring onions (scallions), cut into
   1 cm (½ inch) lengths
ground white pepper, to sprinkle

Serves 4

Take the stems off the dried chillies, cut each chilli into 1 cm (½ inch) pieces with scissors or a sharp knife and discard the seeds.

Mix the fish sauce, oyster sauce, stock and sugar in a small bowl.

Heat the oil in a wok over a medium heat and stir-fry the cashew nuts for 2 to 3 minutes or until light brown. Remove with a slotted spoon and drain on paper towels.

Stir-fry the chillies in the same oil over a medium heat for 1 minute. They should darken but not blacken and burn. Remove with a slotted spoon.

Heat the same oil again and stir-fry half the garlic over a medium heat until light brown. Add half the chicken pieces and stir-fry over a high heat for 4 to 5 minutes or until the chicken is cooked. Remove from the wok and repeat with the remaining garlic and chicken pieces. Return all the chicken to the wok.

Add the capsicum, carrot, onion and the sauce mixture to the wok and stir-fry for 1 to 2 minutes. Taste, then adjust the seasoning if necessary. Add the cashew nuts, chillies and spring onions and toss well. Sprinkle with ground white pepper.

chicken with cashew nuts

chiang mai pork curry

500 g (1 lb 2 oz) pork belly, cut into cubes
2 tablespoons oil
2 garlic cloves, crushed
2 tablespoons Chiang Mai curry paste
   (page 249) or bought paste
4 Asian shallots, smashed with the blade
   of a cleaver
4 cm (1½ inch) piece of ginger, shredded
4 tablespoons roasted unsalted peanuts
3 tablespoons tamarind purée
2 tablespoons fish sauce
2 tablespoons palm sugar

Serves 4

Blanch the pork cubes in boiling water for 1 minute, then drain well.

Heat the oil in a wok or saucepan and fry the garlic for 1 minute. Add the curry paste and stir-fry until fragrant. Add the pork, shallots, ginger and peanuts and stir briefly. Add 500 ml (2 cups) water and the tamarind purée and bring to a boil.

Add the fish sauce and sugar and simmer for about 1½ hours or until the pork is very tender. Add more water as the pork cooks, if necessary. The meat is ready when it is very tender.

2–3 garlic cloves, chopped
1 tablespoon chopped coriander (cilantro)
 roots or ground coriander
6 tablespoons palm sugar
7 tablespoons plum sauce or tomato
 ketchup
2 tablespoons light soy sauce
2 tablespoons oyster sauce
1 teaspoon ground pepper
$^1/_2$ teaspoon ground star anise (optional)
900 g (2 lb) pork spare ribs, chopped into
 13–15 cm (5–6 inch) long pieces (baby
 back, if possible — ask your butcher to
 prepare it)

Serves 4

Using a pestle and mortar or a small blender, pound or blend the garlic and coriander roots into a paste. In a large bowl, combine all the ingredients and rub the marinade all over the ribs with your fingers. Cover with plastic wrap and marinate in the refrigerator for at least 3 hours, or overnight.

Preheat the oven to 180°C/350°F/Gas 4 or heat a barbecue or grill (broiler). If cooking in the oven, place the ribs with all the marinade in a baking dish. Bake for 45 to 60 minutes, basting several times during cooking. If barbecuing, put the ribs on the grill, cover and cook for 45 minutes, turning and basting a couple of times. If the ribs do not go sufficiently brown, grill (broil) them for 5 minutes on each side until well browned and slightly charred. If using a grill, line the grill tray with foil. Cook the pork, turning several times and brushing frequently with the remaining sauce, until the meat is cooked through and slightly charred.

barbecued
pork spare ribs

sliced steak with
hot and sour sauce

350 g (12 oz) lean sirloin, rump or
  fillet steak
2 tablespoons fish sauce
4 tablespoons lime juice
1 teaspoon sugar
¼ teaspoon roasted chilli powder
3–4 Asian shallots, finely sliced
a few lettuce leaves, to serve
20 g (⅓ cup) roughly chopped coriander
  (cilantro) leaves, for garnish
15 g (¼ cup) roughly chopped mint leaves,
  for garnish

Serves 4

Heat a barbecue or grill (broiler) to medium. If using a grill, line the tray
with foil. Put the beef on the grill rack and sprinkle both sides with salt and
pepper. Cook for 5 to 7 minutes on each side, turning occasionally. Fat
should drip off the meat and the meat should cook slowly enough to remain
juicy and not burn. Using a sharp knife, slice the cooked beef crossways
into strips.

Mix the fish sauce, lime juice, sugar and chilli powder in a bowl. Add
the Asian shallots and the slices of beef. Taste, then adjust the seasoning
if necessary.

Line a serving plate with lettuce leaves, then spoon the mixture over the
leaves. Sprinkle with coriander and mint leaves.

60 ml (¼ cup) coconut cream
2 tablespoons red curry paste (page 245)
    or bought paste
3 tablespoons fish sauce
1½ tablespoons palm sugar
500 g (1 lb 2 oz) lean pork, finely sliced
440 ml (1¾ cups) coconut milk
280 g (10 oz) Thai eggplants (aubergines),
    cut in halves or quarters, or 1 eggplant
    (aubergine), cubed
75 g (3 oz) fresh green peppercorns,
    cleaned
7 makrut (kaffir) lime leaves, torn in half
2 long red chillies, seeded and finely
    sliced, for garnish

Serves 4

Put the coconut cream in a wok or saucepan and simmer over a medium heat for about 5 minutes, or until the cream separates and a layer of oil forms on the surface. Stir the cream if it starts to brown around the edges.

Add the curry paste, stir well to combine and cook until fragrant. Add the fish sauce and palm sugar and cook for another 2 minutes or until the mixture begins to darken. Add the pork and stir for 5 to 7 minutes.

Add the coconut milk to the saucepan or wok and simmer over a medium heat for another 5 minutes. Add the eggplants and green peppercorns and cook for 5 minutes. Add the makrut lime leaves. Taste, then adjust the seasoning if necessary. Transfer to a serving bowl and sprinkle with the sliced chilli.

red pork curry with green peppercorns

vermicelli soup
with minced pork

15 pieces of dried black fungus
50 g (2 oz) mung bean vermicelli
2 tablespoons vegetable oil
3–4 large garlic cloves, finely chopped
450 g (1 lb) minced (ground) pork
20 coriander (cilantro) leaves, finely
    chopped
¼ teaspoon salt
¼ teaspoon ground white pepper
625 ml (2½ cups) vegetable or chicken
    stock
2 tablespoons light soy sauce
1 tablespoon preserved radish
a few coriander (cilantro) leaves,
    for garnish

Serves 4

Soak the mushrooms in hot water for 5 minutes or until soft, then drain them and cut into smaller pieces if necessary.

Soak the mung bean vermicelli in hot water for 5 to 7 minutes or until soft, then drain well and cut into small pieces.

Heat the oil in a small wok or frying pan and stir-fry the garlic until light golden. Remove from the heat, lift out the garlic with a slotted spoon and drain on paper towels.

In a bowl, combine the pork with the coriander leaves, salt and pepper. Use a spoon or your wet hands to shape the mixture into small balls about 1 cm (½ inch) across.

Heat the stock to boiling point in a saucepan. Add the light soy sauce and preserved radish. Lower the pork balls into the stock and cook for 2 minutes over a medium heat. Add the mushrooms and noodles and cook for another 1 to 2 minutes, stirring frequently. Taste, then adjust the seasoning if necessary. Sprinkle with crispy garlic, garlic oil and coriander leaves.

curry pastes

The complex, deep flavours found in all Thai curries, *kaeng*, are due not to long, slow cooking times, but to the careful preparation of curry pastes. Dry spices and fresh seasonings are lovingly pounded together in a pestle and mortar for at least 15 to 20 minutes to create an intensely flavoured and aromatic paste, crushed smooth, bound with shrimp paste, then cooked in coconut cream to give Thai curries their distinctively sweet and pungent character.

Whereas Indian curries are flavoured mainly with toasty, dried spices, the curry pastes of Thailand typically combine just a few roasted spices such as cumin, coriander and pepper, with a base of garlic and shallots and a selection of Thailand's signature fresh ingredients: lemon grass, makrut (kaffir) lime leaves and zest, galangal, fresh turmeric and tamarind, chillies and just-picked herbs. The result is a wet paste that gives these curries different layers of flavour and aroma, each one rising to the surface as the curry cooks, from the initial burst of citrus to a final mellow spiciness. Although Thai curries are infamously fiery,

a relatively short cooking time also preserves the intensity of the fresh flavours. Many Thai curries are not hot at all; the word 'kaeng' meaning not a spicy dish but a liquid one, refers also to the blandest of soups.

The most popular Thai curries seem colour-coded, the colour an indication of both taste and heat. Red curry paste is dyed by dried long red chillies and is quite mild. Green curry paste is crushed from fresh green chillies and herbs and is usually very hot, while the yellow paste is the hottest of all, coloured by pale dried bird's eye chillies and the golden-yellow turmeric of the south.

Although called 'curry', the Thai curry does not necessarily have Indian roots at all; possibly only a mutual respect for chilli-hot food links the two. However, the Thai cook has always soaked up foreign ingredients and techniques and in the north, drier Burmese-influenced curries make use of dried spices, while the popular Massaman, Muslim, curries also feature many of the roasted spices so familiar from Indian cooking.

2 pieces of cinnamon stick
10 cardamom seeds
5 cloves
2 tablespoons vegetable oil
2 tablespoons massaman curry paste
    (page 247) or bought paste
800 g (1 lb 12 oz) beef flank or rump
    steak, cut into 5 cm (2 inch) cubes
410 ml (1²/₃ cups) coconut milk
250 ml (1 cup) beef stock
2–3 potatoes, cut into 2.5 cm (1 inch)
    pieces
2 cm (³/₄ inch) piece of ginger, shredded
3 tablespoons fish sauce
3 tablespoons palm sugar
110 g (²/₃ cup) roasted salted peanuts,
    without skin
3 tablespoons tamarind purée

Serves 4

Dry-fry the cinnamon stick, cardamom seeds and cloves in a saucepan or wok over a low heat. Stir all the ingredients around for 2 to 3 minutes or until fragrant. Remove from the pan.

Heat the oil in the same saucepan or wok and stir-fry the massaman paste over a medium heat for 2 minutes or until fragrant.

Add the beef to the pan and stir for 5 minutes. Add the coconut milk, beef stock, potatoes, ginger, fish sauce, palm sugar, three-quarters of the roasted peanuts, tamarind purée and the dry-fried spices. Reduce the heat to low and gently simmer for 50 to 60 minutes until the meat is tender and the potatoes are just cooked. Taste, then adjust the seasoning if necessary. Spoon into a serving bowl and garnish with the rest of the roasted peanuts.

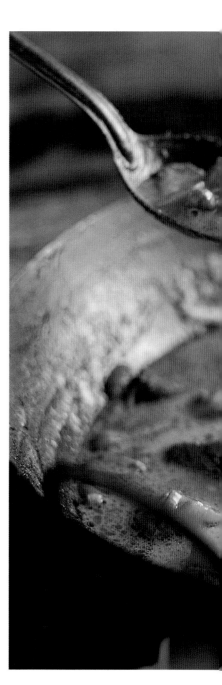

massaman curry with beef

beef with thai sweet basil leaves

1 tablespoon fish sauce
3 tablespoons oyster sauce
4 tablespoons vegetable or chicken stock,
   or water
$^1/_2$ teaspoon sugar
2 tablespoons vegetable oil
4 garlic cloves, finely chopped
3 bird's eye chillies, lightly crushed with
   the side of a cleaver
500 g (1 lb 2 oz) tender rump or fillet
   steak, finely sliced
1 medium onion, cut into thin wedges
2 handfuls of Thai sweet basil leaves

Serves 4

Mix the fish sauce, oyster sauce, stock and sugar in a small bowl.

Heat the oil in the wok or frying pan and stir-fry half the garlic over a medium heat until light brown. Add half the crushed chillies and half the meat and stir-fry over a high heat for 2 to 3 minutes or until the meat is cooked. Remove from the wok and repeat with the remaining garlic, chillies and meat. Return all the meat to the wok.

Add the onion and the fish sauce mixture and stir-fry for another minute.

Add the basil leaves and stir-fry until the basil begins to wilt. Taste, then adjust the seasoning if necessary. Spoon onto a serving plate.

60 ml (¼ cup) coconut cream
2 tablespoons green curry paste
   (page 244) or bought paste
350 g (12 oz) skinless chicken thigh
   fillets, sliced
440 ml (1¾ cups) coconut milk
2½ tablespoons fish sauce
1 tablespoon palm sugar
350 g (12 oz) mixed Thai eggplants
   (aubergines), cut into quarters, and
   pea eggplants (aubergines)
50 g (2 oz) galangal, julienned
7 makrut (kaffir) lime leaves, torn in half
a handful of Thai sweet basil leaves,
   for garnish
1 long red chilli, seeded and finely sliced,
   for garnish

Serves 4

Put the coconut cream in a wok or saucepan and simmer over a medium heat for about 5 minutes, or until the cream separates and a layer of oil forms on the surface. Stir the cream if it starts to brown around the edges. Add the curry paste, stir well to combine and cook until fragrant.

Add the chicken and stir for a few minutes. Add nearly all of the coconut milk, the fish sauce and palm sugar and simmer over a medium heat for another 5 minutes.

Add the eggplants and cook, stirring occasionally, for about 5 minutes or until the eggplants are cooked. Add the galangal and makrut lime leaves. Taste, then adjust the seasoning if necessary. Spoon into a serving bowl and sprinkle with the last bit of coconut milk, as well as the basil leaves and chilli slices.

green curry
with chicken

pork with ginger

15 g (½ oz) dried black fungus
   (about half a handful)
1 tablespoon fish sauce
1½ tablespoons oyster sauce
4 tablespoons vegetable or chicken
   stock, or water
½ teaspoon sugar
2 tablespoons vegetable oil
3–4 garlic cloves, finely chopped
500 g (1 lb 2 oz) lean pork, finely sliced
25 g (1 oz) ginger, julienned
1 small onion, cut into 8 wedges
2 spring onions (scallions), diagonally
   sliced
ground white pepper, for sprinkling
1 long red chilli, seeded and finely sliced,
   for garnish
a few coriander (cilantro) leaves, for
   garnish

Serves 4

Soak the black fungus in hot water for 2 to 3 minutes or until soft, then drain.

Mix the fish sauce, oyster sauce, stock and sugar in a small bowl.

Heat the oil in a wok or frying pan and stir-fry half the garlic over a medium heat until light brown. Add half the pork and stir-fry over a high heat for 2 to 3 minutes or until the pork is cooked. Remove from the wok. Repeat with the remaining garlic and pork. Return all the pork to the wok.

Add the ginger, onion, black fungus and the sauce mixture to the wok. Stir-fry for 1 to 2 minutes. Taste, then adjust the seasoning if necessary. Stir in the spring onions.

Spoon onto a serving plate and sprinkle with ground pepper, chilli slices and coriander leaves.

vegetable oil, for deep-frying
75 g (3 oz) Asian shallots, finely sliced
6 garlic cloves, finely chopped
500 g (1 lb 2 oz) shoulder or leg of pork,
   cut into thin slices
1 tablespoon oyster sauce
1 tablespoon light soy sauce
1 tablespoon fish sauce
4 tablespoons palm sugar
¼ teaspoon ground white pepper

Serves 4

Heat 5 cm (2 inches) oil in a deep saucepan or wok over a medium heat and deep-fry the shallots until they are golden brown. Be careful not to burn them. Remove them from the wok with a slotted spoon and drain well on paper towels.

Drain the oil from the saucepan or wok, leaving 2 tablespoons in the pan. Stir-fry the garlic in the oil until light brown, then add the pork and stir-fry for a few minutes. Add the oyster sauce, light soy sauce, fish sauce, sugar and ground pepper and continue cooking for about 5 minutes, or until all the liquid has evaporated and the mixture forms a thick sticky sauce.

Spoon onto a serving plate and sprinkle with the crispy shallots.

caramel pork

grilled chicken

MARINADE
4 coriander (cilantro) roots, finely chopped
4 garlic cloves, finely chopped
1 lemon grass stalk, white part only,
   finely chopped
3 tablespoons fish sauce
¹/₄ teaspoon ground white pepper
1 teaspoon palm sugar

1 chicken, spatchcocked
sweet chilli sauce, to serve
lime wedges, to serve

Serves 4

Using a pestle and mortar, pound the marinade ingredients together, then spoon into a bowl. Add the chicken and rub the marinade all over the chicken skin. Cover and marinate in the refrigerator for at least 3 hours, or overnight.

Heat a barbecue, char-grill or grill (broiler) until very hot. Cook the chicken for 20 to 30 minutes, turning it over at regular intervals.

Cut the chicken into pieces. Serve with sweet chilli sauce and lime wedges.

500 g (1 lb 2 oz) skinless chicken breast
   fillets, thinly sliced
4–5 garlic cloves, finely chopped
4–5 small red or green bird's eye chillies,
   lightly crushed
1 tablespoon fish sauce
2 tablespoons oyster sauce
vegetable oil, for deep-frying
2 handfuls of holy basil leaves
2 tablespoons vegetable or chicken stock,
   or water
1/2 teaspoon sugar
1 red capsicum (pepper), cut into
   bite-sized pieces
1 medium onion, cut into thin wedges

Serves 4

Mix the chicken, garlic, chillies, fish sauce and oyster sauce in a bowl.
Cover with plastic wrap and marinate in the refrigerator for at least
30 minutes.

Heat 5 cm (2 inches) oil in a wok or deep frying pan over a medium heat.
When the oil seems hot, drop a few basil leaves into it. If they sizzle
immediately, the oil is ready. Deep-fry three-quarters of the basil leaves for
1 minute or until they are crispy. Lift out with a slotted spoon and drain on
paper towels. Discard the remaining oil.

Heat 2 tablespoons oil in the same wok or frying pan and stir-fry half the
chicken over a high heat for 3 to 4 minutes. Remove from the pan and
repeat with the remaining chicken. Return all the chicken to the wok.

Add the stock and sugar to the wok, then the capsicum and onion, and
stir-fry for another 1 to 2 minutes. Stir in the fresh basil leaves. Taste, then
adjust the seasoning if necessary. Garnish with the crispy basil leaves.

chicken with crispy holy basil leaves

naam phrik (chilli sauce)...

Naam phrik, literally 'spicy water', is a chilli dip or relish and a particularly Thai creation. Whereas in other cuisines where such relishes are an accompaniment or seasoning, *naam phrik* is always at the centre of a meal, the accompaniments chosen to complement the dip in flavour and texture.

Naam phrik can be pungent, hot or smoky, but its taste is always strong. Perhaps the quintessential Thai dish, the dip balances distinct sour, spicy and salty flavours with an edge of sweetness, with the underlying fermented flavour of roasted shrimp paste richly binding everything together. When coconut cream is added, the sauces are known as *lon* and are sweeter, and usually have a more fermented taste.

Condiments for dipping include crisp raw vegetables, such as cucumber, cabbage and green beans; deep-fried pumpkin, aubergine (eggplant) or sweet potato; an omelette; grilled seafood and chicken or deep-fried pork rind; and fruit and blossoms. In hard times, just a little *naam phrik* stirred into rice was seen as a meal in itself.

panaeng beef curry

2 tablespoons vegetable oil
2 tablespoons dry curry paste (page 248)
    or bought paste
700 g (1 lb 9 oz) beef flank steak, sliced
    into strips
185 ml (¾ cup) coconut milk
1 tablespoon fish sauce
1 tablespoon palm sugar
3 tablespoons tamarind purée
2 makrut (kaffir) lime leaves, finely sliced,
    for garnish
½ long red chilli, seeded and finely sliced,
    for garnish
cucumber relish (page 251), to serve

Serves 4

Heat the oil in a saucepan or wok and stir-fry the curry paste over a medium heat for 2 minutes or until fragrant.

Add the beef and stir for 5 minutes. Add nearly all of the coconut milk, the fish sauce, palm sugar and tamarind purée and reduce to a low heat. Simmer, uncovered, for 5 to 7 minutes. Although this is meant to be a dry curry, you can add a little more water during cooking if you feel it is drying out too much. Taste, then adjust the seasoning if necessary.

Spoon the curry into a serving bowl, spoon the last bit of coconut milk over the top and sprinkle with makrut lime leaves and chilli slices. Serve with cucumber relish.

12 raw small prawns (shrimp), peeled, deveined and roughly chopped
1 lemon grass stalk, white part only, finely chopped
2 large green chillies, chopped
1 teaspoon Thai whisky or rice wine
1 teaspoon fish sauce
1 teaspoon tapioca flour
2 garlic cloves, chopped
2 coriander (cilantro) roots, chopped

2 cm (¾ inch) piece of ginger, chopped
2 Asian shallots, chopped
200 g (1 cup) jasmine rice
2 tablespoons oil
2 Thai or Chinese sour sausages, finely sliced
2 tablespoons chopped coriander (cilantro), for garnish

Serves 4

Put the chopped prawns in a bowl with 1 tablespoon of lemon grass, the chillies, whisky, fish sauce and tapioca flour. Stir to combine.

Pound the remaining lemon grass, garlic, coriander roots, ginger and Asian shallots in a pestle and mortar or blend in a small food processor to form a rough paste.

Wash the rice in cold water until the water runs clear, then drain.

Heat the oil in a wok, add the garlic paste and cook for 3 to 4 minutes, stirring constantly. Add the rice and cook for a minute to coat the rice evenly in the mixture.

Transfer the rice into a large clay pot and add enough water so there is 2 cm (¾ inch) of water above the surface of the rice. Bring the water to a slow boil, then place the sausage slices on top of the rice and the prawn mixture on top of the sausages. Cover the clay pot and cook over a low heat for 15 minutes or until the rice is cooked. Sprinkle with the chopped coriander and serve.

prawns and sausage
in a clay pot

pork with snake beans

1 tablespoon oyster sauce
1 tablespoon light soy sauce
¼ teaspoon sugar
2 tablespoons vegetable oil
4 garlic cloves, finely chopped
350 g (12 oz) pork fillet, finely sliced
250 g (9 oz) snake beans, cut into 5 cm
   (2 inch) pieces
½ long red chilli, seeded, shredded,
   for garnish (optional)

Serves 4

Mix the oyster sauce, light soy sauce, sugar and 2 tablespoons water in a small bowl.

Heat the oil in a wok or frying pan and stir-fry the garlic over a medium heat until light brown. Add the pork and stir-fry over a high heat for 3 to 5 minutes or until the pork is cooked. Add the beans and the sauce mixture and stir-fry for 4 minutes. Taste, then adjust the seasoning if necessary.

Transfer to a serving plate and garnish with chilli slices.

2 teaspoons fish sauce
2 tablespoons oyster sauce
60 ml (¼ cup) coconut milk
½ teaspoon sugar
2½ tablespoons vegetable oil
6 garlic cloves, finely chopped
1–1½ tablespoons chilli jam (page 250),
**   to taste**
500 g (1 lb 2 oz) skinless chicken breast
**   fillets, finely sliced**
a handful of holy basil leaves
1 long red or green chilli, seeded and finely
**   sliced, for garnish**

Serves 4

Mix the fish sauce, oyster sauce, coconut milk and sugar in a small bowl.

Heat the oil in a wok or frying pan and stir-fry half the garlic over a medium heat until light brown. Add half the chilli jam and stir-fry for another 2 minutes or until fragrant. Add half of the chicken and stir-fry over a high heat for 2 to 3 minutes. Remove from the wok. Repeat with the remaining garlic, chilli jam and chicken. Return all the chicken to the wok.

Add the fish sauce mixture to the wok and stir-fry for a few more seconds or until the chicken is cooked. Taste, then adjust the seasoning if necessary. Stir in the basil leaves. Garnish with chilli slices.

chicken with chilli jam

green papaya salad

120 g (4 oz) small hard, green, unripe
   papaya
1½ tablespoons palm sugar
1 tablespoon fish sauce
1–2 garlic cloves
25 g (1 oz) roasted peanuts
25 g (1 oz) snake beans, cut into 2.5 cm
   (1 inch) pieces
1 tablespoon ground dried shrimp
2–6 bird's eye chillies, stems removed
   (6 will give a very hot result)
50 g (2 oz) cherry tomatoes, left whole,
   or 2 medium tomatoes, cut into
   6 wedges
half a lime
sticky rice (page 243), to serve

Serves 1

Peel the green papaya with a vegetable peeler and cut the papaya into long, thin shreds. If you have a mandolin, use the grater attachment.

Mix the palm sugar with the fish sauce until the sugar has dissolved.

Using a large, deep pestle and mortar, pound the garlic into a paste. Add the roasted peanuts and pound roughly together with the garlic. Add the papaya and pound softly, using a spoon to scrape down the sides, and turning and mixing well.

Add the beans, dried shrimp and chillies and keep pounding and turning to bruise these ingredients. Add the sugar mixture and tomatoes, squeeze in the lime juice and add the lime skin to the mixture. Lightly pound together for another minute until thoroughly mixed. As the juice comes out, pound more gently so the liquid doesn't splash. Discard the lime skin. Taste the sauce in the bottom of the mortar and adjust the seasoning if necessary. It should be a balance of sweet and sour with a hot and salty taste.

Spoon the papaya salad and all the juices onto a serving plate. Serve with sticky rice.

a little taste of...

Thailand's long southern tail offers kilometres of coastline fringing the warm, seafood-rich waters of the Gulf of Thailand. Fresh fish is therefore one of the joys of Thai cooking, relatively inexpensive and eaten at almost every meal, especially in the south. Even in the landlocked North, the country is endowed with plentiful fresh-water fish, the most amateur fisherman able to land a catch from the country's extensive network of streams, rivers, ponds, even paddy fields and monsoon-filled puddles.

Fish tends to be served whole. When very fresh, it may simply be steamed or grilled with chilli, lime juice or ginger. It is also roasted, sometimes wrapped in banana leaves, or fried crisp and smothered with a sauce. Seafood can be stir-fried with roasted chilli, garlic or herbs, and also turns up in all kinds of dishes, notably in Thailand's wonderful hot and sour seafood salads.

The Thais also love to salt, dry and pickle seafood, both to preserve it and to add extra punch. Even meat and vegetable dishes have a taste of the sea thanks to the essential seasonings of shrimp paste and fish sauce.

...the sea

150 g (5 oz) vermicelli or mung bean
    vermicelli (*wun sen*)
280 g (10 oz) raw medium prawns
    (shrimp)
920 ml (3²/₃ cups) vegetable stock
2 lemon grass stalks, each cut into a
    tassel or bruised
2–2¹/₂ tablespoons fish sauce
1¹/₂–2 tablespoons chilli jam (page 250),
    to taste (optional)
1–2 small red and green chillies, slightly
    crushed
110 g (4 oz) mixed mushrooms
110 g (4 oz) baby tomatoes (about 10) or
    medium tomatoes, cut into 6 pieces
5 makrut (kaffir) lime leaves, torn in half
4 tablespoons lime juice
a few coriander (cilantro) leaves, for
    garnish

Serves 4

Soak the vermicelli in hot water for 1 to 2 minutes or until soft, then drain
them well and cut into small pieces.

Peel and devein the prawns and cut each prawn along the back so it opens
like a butterfly (leave each prawn joined along the base and at the tail,
leaving the tail attached).

Heat the stock, lemon grass, fish sauce, chilli jam and crushed chillies to
boiling point. Reduce the heat to medium, add the vermicelli and cook for
1 to 2 minutes. Add the prawns and cook for another minute.

Add the mushrooms, tomatoes, makrut lime leaves and lime juice. Cook for
another 2 to 3 minutes, taking care not to let the tomatoes lose their shape.
Taste, then adjust the seasoning if necessary. Discard the lemon grass.
Spoon into a bowl and garnish with coriander leaves.

hot and sour soup with noodles and prawns

sticky rice with shrimp or coconut topping

SHRIMP TOPPING
2 garlic cloves, roughly chopped
4 coriander (cilantro) roots, cleaned
¼ teaspoon ground black pepper
1 tablespoon vegetable oil
200 g (7 oz) minced (ground) shrimp
    or very small raw prawns (shrimp)
25 g (1 oz) grated coconut
1 teaspoon fish sauce
3 tablespoons sugar

OR

COCONUT TOPPING
150 g (5 oz) grated coconut or desiccated
    coconut
150 g (5 oz) palm sugar

1 quantity of sticky rice with coconut milk
    (page 243)
3 makrut (kaffir) lime leaves, finely sliced,
    for garnish

Serves 4

To make the shrimp topping, use a pestle and mortar to pound the garlic, coriander roots and pepper to a smooth paste. Alternatively, chop with a sharp knife until smooth. Heat the oil in a wok or frying pan and stir-fry the garlic mixture over a medium heat until fragrant. Add the minced shrimp or prawns, coconut, fish sauce and sugar and stir-fry for 3 to 4 minutes or until the minced shrimp is cooked. Taste, then adjust the seasoning if necessary. The flavour should be sweet and lightly salty.

To make the coconut topping, mix the coconut, sugar, 125 ml (½ cup) water and a pinch of salt in a saucepan and stir over a low heat until the sugar is dissolved. Do not let it thicken to a point where it will harden. Remove from the heat.

Serve by filling a small, wet bowl with the sticky rice and turning it out on a small dessert plate. Top with shrimp or coconut topping and a sprinkle of lime leaves. You can use half of each topping if you like.

banana leaves
2 handfuls of Thai sweet basil leaves
fish filling (page 67)
2 tablespoons coconut cream
3–4 makrut (kaffir) lime leaves, finely
   sliced
1 long red chilli, seeded and finely sliced,
   for garnish

Makes 6 banana cups

To **soften** the banana leaves and prevent them splitting, put them in a hot oven for about 10 to 20 seconds, or blanch them briefly. Cut the leaves into 12 circles 15 cm (6 inches) in diameter with the fibre running lengthways. Place one piece with the fibre running lengthways and another on top with the fibre running across. Make a 1 cm ($^1/_2$ inch) deep tuck 4 cm (1$^1/_2$ inches) long (4 cm (1$^1/_2$ inches) in from the edge and no further) and pin securely with a small sharp toothpick. Repeat at the opposite point and at the two side points, making four tucks altogether. Flatten the base as best you can. Repeat to make 6 square-shaped cups. Place a few basil leaves in the bottom of each cup and spoon in the fish filling until three-quarters full.

Fill a wok or a steamer pan with water, cover and bring to a boil over a high heat. Place the banana cups on a plate. Use a plate that will fit on the rack of a traditional bamboo steamer basket or on a steamer rack inside the wok or pan. (If your wok or pan has a special steaming plate that will hold the cups flat, you may not need to put them on a separate plate.) Taking care not to burn your hands, set the rack or basket over the water and put the plate on the rack. Reduce the heat to a simmer. Cover and cook for 15 to 20 minutes. Check and replenish the water after 10 minutes.

When the cups are cooked the filling will puff and rise slightly. Turn off the heat and carefully transfer the cups to a serving plate. Spoon a little coconut cream on top and sprinkle with lime leaves and sliced chilli.

fish steamed in banana leaf

jungle curry
with prawns

JUNGLE CURRY PASTE
8 bird's eye chillies, chopped
2 cm (¾ inch) piece of galangal, chopped
2 lemon grass stalks, white part only,
    finely chopped
4 Asian shallots, finely chopped
4 garlic cloves, finely sliced
½ teaspoon shrimp paste

400 g (14 oz) raw prawns (shrimp)
1 tablespoon oil
4 baby sweet corn, each cut into half
    lengthways on an angle

75 g (3 oz) Thai eggplants (aubergines),
    cut in halves or quarters
50 g (2 oz) pea eggplants (aubergines)
50 g (2 oz) straw or button mushrooms,
    halved if large
1 tablespoon fish sauce
½ teaspoon palm sugar
2–3 makrut (kaffir) lime leaves, torn into
    pieces, for garnish
a handful of holy basil or Thai sweet basil
    leaves, for garnish

Serves 4

Put all the jungle curry paste ingredients in a pestle and mortar and pound until smooth. Alternatively, put them in a food processor with 2 tablespoons water and process to a smooth paste.

Peel and devein the prawns and cut each prawn along the back so it opens like a butterfly (leave each prawn joined along the base and at the tail).

Heat the oil in a wok or saucepan and stir-fry 2 tablespoons of the curry paste until fragrant. Add 410 ml (1⅔ cups) water and reduce the heat to medium. Add the sweet corn and eggplants and cook for 1 to 2 minutes. Add the mushrooms and prawns, fish sauce and sugar. Cook until the prawns open and turn pink. Taste, then adjust the seasoning if necessary. Sprinkle with the makrut lime leaves and basil leaves before serving.

450 g (1 lb) mussels or clams in the shell
1½ tablespoons vegetable oil
2–3 garlic cloves, finely chopped
1 small onion, finely chopped
3 lemon grass stalks, white part only,
    finely sliced
2.5 cm (1 inch) piece of galangal, cut into
    7–8 slices
2 long red chillies, seeded and finely
    chopped
1 tablespoon fish sauce
1 tablespoon lime juice
½ teaspoon sugar
25 g (1 cup) holy basil leaves,
    roughly chopped

Serves 2

Scrub the mussels or clams and remove any hairy beards from the mussels.
Discard any open mussels or clams and any that don't close when tapped on
the work surface. If using clams, wash them in several changes of cold water
until the water is clear, then put them in a large bowl, cover with cold water
and soak for 30 minutes. This helps remove the sand from the clams.

Heat the oil in a wok and stir-fry the garlic, onion, lemon grass, galangal
and chillies over a medium heat for 1 to 2 minutes or until fragrant.

Add the mussels or clams and stir-fry for a few minutes. Add the fish sauce,
lime juice and sugar. Cover loosely and cook over a medium heat for
5 to 7 minutes, shaking the wok frequently. Cook until the shells are open,
discarding any unopened shells. Mix in the chopped holy basil. Taste,
then adjust the seasoning if necessary. Serve hot in a large bowl.

mussels with lemon grass

crispy fish salad

DRESSING
1 lemon grass stalk, white part only, roughly chopped
4 bird's eye chillies, stems removed
1 garlic clove, chopped
1 tablespoon fish sauce
2 tablespoons lime juice
2 teaspoons palm sugar
¼ teaspoon ground turmeric

300 g (10 oz) skinless firm white fish fillets

1 tablespoon sea salt
peanut oil, for deep-frying
3 tomatoes or large cherry tomatoes, each cut into 4 or 6 wedges
2 Asian shallots, thinly sliced
1 small red onion, sliced into thin wedges
15 g (½ cup) coriander (cilantro) leaves
18–24 mint leaves
2 tablespoons roasted peanuts, roughly chopped

Serves 4

To make the dressing, use a pestle and mortar or food processor to pound or blend the lemon grass, chillies and garlic to a paste. Transfer to a bowl and add the fish sauce, lime juice, palm sugar and turmeric. Stir until the sugar dissolves.

Preheat the oven to 180°C/350°F/Gas 4. Pat dry the fish fillets, then toss them in the sea salt. Place them on a rack in a baking tray and bake for 20 minutes. Remove, allow to cool, then transfer to a food processor and chop until the fish resembles large breadcrumbs.

Half fill a wok with oil and heat over a high heat. Drop a small piece of fish into the oil. If it sizzles immediately, the oil is ready. Drop a large handful of the chopped fish into the hot oil. The fish will puff up and turn crisp. Cook for 30 seconds and carefully stir a little. Cook for another 30 seconds until golden brown. Remove with a slotted spoon and drain on paper towels. Repeat to cook all the fish.

Put the tomatoes, shallots, red onion, coriander leaves, mint leaves and peanuts in a bowl with about half of the dressing. Transfer the salad to a serving plate. Break the fish into smaller pieces if you wish and place on the salad. To ensure that the fish stays crispy, pour the remaining dressing over the salad just before serving.

**4 red tilapa, grey/red mullet, or mackerel
  (about 300 g/10 oz each)**
8–10 garlic cloves, roughly chopped
6 coriander (cilantro) roots, chopped
1 teaspoon ground white pepper
1 teaspoon salt
1 tablespoon vegetable oil
8 pieces of banana leaf
a chilli sauce, to serve

Serves 4

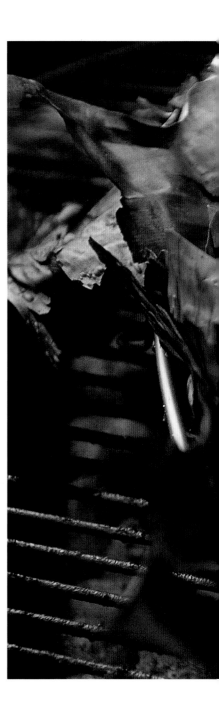

Clean and gut the fish, leaving the heads on. Dry the fish thoroughly. Score each fish three or four times on both sides with a sharp knife.

Using a pestle and mortar or a small blender, pound or blend the garlic, coriander roots, ground pepper, salt and oil into a paste. Rub the garlic paste inside the cavities and all over each fish. Cover and marinate in the refrigerator for at least 30 minutes.

To soften the banana leaves and prevent them from splitting, put them in a hot oven for 10 to 20 seconds, or blanch them briefly. Using two pieces of banana leaf, each with the grain running at right angles to the other, wrap each fish like a parcel. Pin the ends of the banana leaves together with toothpicks.

Heat a grill (broiler) or barbecue to medium. Barbecue or grill (broil) the fish for about 15 minutes on each side or until the fish is light brown and cooked. To make the fish easier to lift and turn during cooking, you can place the fish in a fish-shaped griddle that opens out like tongs. Transfer the fish to a serving plate. Serve with a chilli sauce.

grilled fish with
garlic and coriander

stuffed squid soup

280 g (10 oz) small squid
2 coriander (cilantro) roots, finely chopped
3–4 large garlic cloves, roughly chopped
280 g (10 oz) minced (ground) pork or
   chicken
¼ teaspoon salt
¼ teaspoon ground white pepper
2 litres (8 cups) vegetable stock
2.5 cm (1 inch) piece of ginger, sliced

4 tablespoons light soy sauce
1 tablespoon preserved radish, sliced
5 spring onions (scallions), slivered,
   for garnish
a few coriander (cilantro) leaves, for
   garnish
ground white pepper, for sprinkling

Serves 4

To clean each squid, grasp the squid body in one hand and pull away the head and tentacles from the body. Cut the head off the tentacles just above the eyes and discard the head. Clean out the body. Pull the skin off the squid and rinse well. Drain well.

Using a pestle and mortar, pound the coriander roots and garlic into a paste. In a bowl, combine the coriander paste with the pork or chicken and the salt and pepper. Spoon some mixture into a squid sac until two-thirds full, being careful not to overfill it as the filling will swell during cooking. Squeeze the squid tube closed at the end. With a bamboo stick or sharp toothpick, prick several holes in the body of the squid. Place on a plate and repeat with the rest. Use a spoon or your wet fingers to shape the remaining meat mixture into small balls about 1 cm (½ inch) across.

Heat the stock to boiling point in a saucepan. Reduce the heat to low and add the ginger, light soy sauce and preserved radish. Lower the meatballs into the stock, then gently drop in the stuffed squid and cook over a low heat for 4 to 5 minutes or until the meatballs and squid are cooked. Taste the broth and adjust the seasoning if necessary.

Garnish with spring onions and coriander leaves. Sprinkle with ground white pepper and serve.

shrimp paste and fish sauce...

In the spectrum of Thai flavours, it is shrimp paste, *ka-pi*, and fish sauce, *naam plaa*, that give Thai cooking its salty taste. Not just salty, but a complex sea-salt flavour, these essences by and large take the place of the table salt used in European cookery and the soy sauce favoured by many other Asian countries.

The two flavourings share common roots and their taste is unmistakeably 'Thai'. Fish sauce is the liquid drained from salted, fermented small fish dried out in the sun, while the residue of a similar process involving shrimp can be made into shrimp paste.

Although the odour can be unappealing, when used in cooking shrimp paste adds powerful depth and flavour. The paste is used to bind together curry pastes and dominates the distinctly Thai *naam phrik* dips.

Fish sauce is poured into almost every dish and is the main ingredient in most of the dipping sauces added at the table for saltiness. Although initially off-putting, the sauce's pungent aroma and taste mellow when combined with other ingredients. *Naam plaa raa* is a northern version made from fermented freshwater fish, its strongly fishy taste reminiscent of the more intense pastes of the past.

500 g (1 lb 2 oz) large raw prawns
  (shrimp)
18–20 coriander (cilantro) roots,
  roughly chopped
4–5 garlic cloves, roughly chopped
10 black peppercorns
1 tablespoon light soy sauce
1½ tablespoons oyster sauce
½ teaspoon sugar
3 tablespoons vegetable oil
a few coriander (cilantro) leaves,
  for garnish
1 long red chilli, seeded and finely sliced,
  for garnish

Serves 4

Peel and devein the prawns and cut each prawn along the back so it opens like a butterfly (leave each prawn joined along the base and at the tail).

Using a pestle and mortar or a small blender, pound or grind the coriander roots and garlic into a rough paste. Add the peppercorns and continue to grind roughly.

Mix the light soy sauce, oyster sauce and sugar in a small bowl.

Heat the oil in a wok or frying pan and stir-fry the coriander paste for 1 to 2 minutes or until the garlic starts to turn light brown and becomes fragrant. Add the prawns and light soy sauce mixture and stir-fry for another 2 to 3 minutes or until the prawns open and turn pink. Taste, then adjust the seasoning if necessary. Sprinkle with coriander leaves and chilli slices.

stir-fried garlic prawns

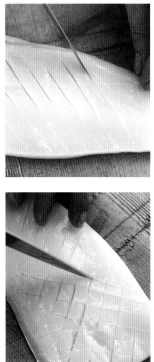

egg noodles
with seafood

8 raw prawns (shrimp)
2 squid tubes
250 g (9 oz) egg noodles
1 tablespoon vegetable oil
4 Asian shallots, smashed with the side
   of a cleaver
4 spring onions (scallions), cut into lengths
   and smashed with the side of a cleaver
2 cm (¾ inch) piece of ginger, finely
   shredded
2 garlic cloves, finely sliced
1 tablespoon preserved cabbage, rinsed
   and chopped (optional)
4 scallops, cut in half horizontally
1 tablespoon oyster sauce
2 teaspoons soy sauce
2 teaspoons fish sauce
½ bunch (1 cup) holy basil leaves

Serves 4

Peel and devein the prawns and cut each prawn along the back so it opens like a butterfly (leave each prawn joined along the base and at the tail, leaving the tail attached).

Open out the squid tubes and score the insides in a criss-cross pattern. Cut the squid tubes into squares.

Cook the egg noodles in boiling water, then drain and rinse.

Heat the oil in a wok and add the shallots, spring onions, ginger, garlic and cabbage and stir-fry for 2 minutes. Add the prawns, squid and scallops one after the other, tossing after each addition, and cook for 3 minutes.

Add the oyster and soy sauces and noodles and toss together. Add the fish sauce and holy basil and serve.

1 large or 2 smaller red snapper (total
   weight about 1 kg/2 lb 4 oz)
3 tablespoons plain (all-purpose) flour
pinch of ground black pepper
1½ tablespoons vegetable oil
½ tablespoon red curry paste (page 245)
   or bought paste
2 tablespoons palm sugar
2 tablespoons fish sauce

vegetable oil, for deep-frying
a handful of Thai sweet basil leaves
1 dried long red chilli, cut into 5 mm
   (¼ inch) pieces, seeds discarded
3 makrut (kaffir) lime leaves, very finely
   sliced, for garnish

Serves 4

Clean and gut the fish, leaving the head/s on. Thoroughly dry the fish.
Score the fish three or four times on both sides with a sharp knife. Rub the
fish inside and out with a pinch of salt. Place the flour and ground pepper
on a plate and press the fish lightly into it until coated with flour from head
to tail. Shake off any excess.

Heat the oil in a small saucepan, add the red curry paste and stir over a
medium heat for 1 to 2 minutes or until fragrant. Add the sugar, fish sauce
and 2 tablespoons water and cook for another 1 to 2 minutes or until the
sugar has dissolved. Remove from the heat.

Heat 10 cm (4 inches) oil in a large wok or pan big enough to deep-fry the
whole fish. When the oil is hot, drop a few basil leaves into it. If they sizzle
immediately, the oil is ready. Deep-fry half of the basil leaves for 1 minute
or until they are all crispy. Remove with a slotted spoon and drain on paper
towels. Deep-fry the rest.

In the same wok, deep-fry the dried chilli pieces for a few seconds over a
medium heat until light brown. Be careful not to burn them. Remove with a
slotted spoon and drain on paper towels. Gently slide the fish into the oil
(be careful as the hot oil may splash). Deep-fry the fish on just one side (but
make sure the oil covers the whole fish) for about 5 to 10 minutes or until
the fish is cooked and light brown (if you cook the fish until it is very brown,
it will be too dry). Drain off the oil and drain the fish on paper towels.

Put the curry sauce in the wok and gently warm it. Add the fish and coat both
sides with the sauce. Transfer the fish to a warm plate with any remaining
sauce and sprinkle with crispy basil, fried chilli pieces and the lime leaves.

deep-fried fish with chillies and basil

hot and sour vermicelli with mixed seafood

110 g (4 oz) mung bean vermicelli
15 g (½ oz) dried black fungus
175 g (6 oz) mixed raw medium prawns
   (shrimp), squid tubes and scallops
8 mussels
1½ tablespoons vegetable oil
4–5 garlic cloves, finely chopped
3 tablespoons lime juice
1 tablespoon fish sauce
2 lemon grass stalks, white part only,
   finely sliced

3 Asian shallots, finely sliced
¼–½ teaspoon chilli powder or
   2–3 bird's eye chillies, finely sliced
3 spring onions (scallions), finely chopped
a few lettuce leaves
1 long red chilli, seeded and finely sliced,
   for garnish

Serves 4

Soak the mung bean vermicelli in boiling water for 1 to 2 minutes or until soft, then drain and roughly chop. Soak the black fungus in boiling water for 2 to 3 minutes or until soft, then drain and roughly chop them.

Peel and devein the prawns and cut each prawn along the back so it opens like a butterfly (leave each prawn joined along the base and at the tail, leaving the tail attached). Peel off the skin from the squid tubes, rinse the insides and cut the tubes into 5 mm (¼ inch) rings. Remove any dark vein from the scallops.

Scrub the mussels and remove their hairy beards. Discard any open mussels and any that don't close when tapped on the work surface.

Heat the oil in a small wok or frying pan and stir the garlic over a medium heat until light brown. Transfer the fried garlic to a small bowl.

In a saucepan or wok, cook the prawns, squid rings and mussels over a medium heat with the lime juice and fish sauce for 1 to 2 minutes or until the prawns open and turn pink. Add the scallops and cook for 1 minute. Discard any unopened mussels. Add the vermicelli and mushrooms to the pan and cook for another 2 minutes or until the vermicelli is cooked. Remove from the heat. Add the lemon grass, shallots, chilli powder or chillies, and spring onions and mix well. Taste, then adjust the seasoning if necessary.

Line a serving plate with lettuce leaves, then spoon the seafood over the leaves. Sprinkle with chilli slices and the fried garlic.

225 g (8 oz) raw prawns (shrimp)
3 tablespoons vegetable oil
4 garlic cloves, finely chopped
1 small onion, sliced
3 teaspoons chilli jam (page 250)
450 g (1 lb) cooked jasmine rice,
    refrigerated overnight
1 tablespoon light soy sauce
1/2 teaspoon sugar
1 long red chilli, seeded and finely sliced
2 spring onions (scallions), finely sliced
ground white pepper, for sprinkling
a few coriander (cilantro) leaves, for
    garnish

Serves 4

Peel and devein the prawns and cut each prawn along the back so it opens like a butterfly (leave each prawn joined along the base and at the tail, leaving the tail attached).

Heat the oil in a wok or frying pan and stir-fry the garlic and onion over a medium heat until light brown. Add the chilli jam and stir for a few seconds or until fragrant. Add the prawns and stir-fry over a high heat for 2 minutes or until the prawns open and turn pink. Add the cooked rice, light soy sauce and sugar and stir-fry for 3 to 4 minutes. Add the chilli and spring onions and mix well. Taste, then adjust the seasoning if necessary.

Spoon onto a serving plate and sprinkle with the ground white pepper and coriander leaves.

fried rice with prawns and chilli jam

deep-fried fish with ginger

15 g (½ oz) dried black fungus (about half a handful)
1 large or 2 smaller red snapper, grey mullet, sea bass or grouper (total weight about 1 kg/2 lb 4 oz)
3 tablespoons plain (all-purpose) flour
pinch of ground black pepper
1 tablespoon oyster sauce
1 tablespoon light soy sauce
¼ teaspoon sugar

vegetable oil, for deep-frying
1½ tablespoons vegetable oil
4 garlic cloves, roughly chopped
1 small carrot, cut into matchsticks
2 cm (¾ inch) piece of ginger, cut into matchsticks
2 spring onions (scallions), finely sliced, for garnish

Serves 4

Soak the black fungus in hot water for 2 to 3 minutes until soft, then drain the fungus and finely chop.

Clean and gut the fish, leaving the head/s on. Dry the fish thoroughly. Score the fish three or four times on both sides with a sharp knife. Rub the fish inside and out with a pinch of salt. Put the flour and ground pepper on a plate and lightly press the fish into it until it is coated all over. Shake off any excess flour.

Mix the oyster sauce, light soy sauce, sugar and 2 tablespoons water in a small bowl.

Heat 10 cm (4 inches) oil in a large wok or saucepan big enough to deep-fry the whole fish. When the oil seems hot, drop a small piece of spring onion into the oil. If it sizzles straight away, the oil is ready. Lower the heat to medium and gently slide the fish into the oil. Be careful as the hot oil may splash. Deep-fry the fish on just one side (but make sure the oil covers the whole fish) for about 5 to 10 minutes or until the fish is cooked and light brown (if you cook the fish until it is very brown, the fish will be too dry). Drain on paper towels before transferring to a warm plate. Keep warm. Drain off the oil.

Heat 1½ tablespoons clean oil in the same wok and stir-fry the garlic over a medium heat until light brown. Add the carrot, ginger, mushrooms and the sauce mixture and stir-fry for 1 to 2 minutes. Taste, then adjust the seasoning if necessary. Pour over the warm fish and sprinkle with spring onions.

1 teaspoon salt
1 teaspoon ground turmeric
1 small green banana or plantain,
  thinly sliced
60 ml (¼ cup) coconut cream
2 tablespoons yellow curry paste
  (page 246) or bought paste
1 tablespoon fish sauce
1 teaspoon palm sugar
400 g (14 oz) snapper or other white
  fish fillets, cut into large cubes
310 ml (1¼ cups) coconut milk
1 small green mango, cut into thin slices
1 large green chilli, finely sliced
12 Thai sweet basil leaves

Serves 4

Bring a small saucepan of water to the boil. Add the salt, turmeric and banana slices and simmer for 10 minutes, then drain.

Put the coconut cream in a wok or saucepan and simmer over a medium heat for about 5 minutes, or until the cream separates and a layer of oil forms on the surface. Stir the cream if it starts to brown around the edges. Add the curry paste, stir well to combine and cook until fragrant. Add the fish sauce and sugar and cook for 2 minutes or until the mixture begins to darken.

Add the fish pieces and stir well to coat the fish in the curry mixture. Slowly add the coconut milk until it has all been incorporated.

Add the banana, mango, green chilli and most of the basil leaves to the wok or pan and gently stir to combine all the ingredients, cooking for a minute or two. Garnish with the remaining basil.

snapper with green
banana and mango

hot and sour noodles with prawns

200 g (7 oz) mung bean vermicelli
100 g (3½ oz) minced (ground) pork
2 tablespoons oil
8 cooked prawns (shrimp), peeled
4 pickled garlic cloves, chopped
2 Asian shallots, finely sliced
4 bird's eye chillies, finely sliced
2 tablespoons fish sauce
1 tablespoon lime juice
2 tomatoes, seeded and cut into thin
   wedges
½ bunch (1 cup) Thai sweet basil leaves
½ bunch (1 cup) coriander (cilantro) leaves

Serves 4

Soak the noodles in hot water for 10 minutes or until soft. Drain the noodles and cut them into shorter lengths using a pair of scissors.

Cook the pork in boiling water for 2 minutes, breaking it up into small pieces, then drain.

Heat the oil in a wok and add all the ingredients except the Thai basil and coriander. Toss together for a minute or two. Add the herbs, toss briefly and serve.

rice... Like many Asians, the Thais consider a meal a meal only if it is served with rice, *khao*. Rice and food are synonymous and, with the exception of snacks, Thai dishes are generally thought of in terms of the flavours and nutrients they add to plain rice. Rice makes up the biggest proportion of the meal; a first mouthful is savoured before any of the other dishes are tasted, and then just a little of each dish is added to flavour it.

The long-grain jasmine rice grown in Thailand is one of the most highly regarded in the world, the Thais themselves calling cooked rice, *khao suay*, 'beautiful rice'. Treated simply, the rice is usually steamed to a fluffy yet not sticky texture and

releases a delicate aroma, though not a floral one, the 'jasmine' referring to the appearance not the fragrance of the rice. It provides a neutral palate to balance the power of Thai dishes.

Thailand is also one of the few countries to value sticky long-grain rice. The rest of Asia rarely uses sticky rice, and then mostly for sweet dishes. Only in the relatively infertile mountains of northern Thailand, Vietnam, Cambodia and Laos where it flourishes is this ancient grain still used as a staple.

Black sticky rice is also popular and while other cuisines shun black food, the Thais have embraced this earthy tasting rice, which combines so well with sugar to become a sweet dish.

At the table, Thai rice is served much hotter than in many other Asian countries, and usually kept warm in a covered basket, a spoonful served out onto the plate only when needed. Sticky rice is traditionally served in a beautiful bamboo basket to keep it warm and moist, and it is always eaten with the fingers, rolled up into a ball and dipped into sauces or consumed with dishes. This versatile rice is also transformed into sweets, usually combined with coconut, as in the banana leaf parcels of sticky sweet rice sold on the streets.

60 ml (¼ cup) coconut cream
2 tablespoons red curry paste (page 245)
    or bought paste
440 ml (1¾ cups) coconut milk
1½–2 tablespoons palm sugar
3 tablespoons fish sauce
350 g (12 oz) skinless firm white fish
    fillets, cut into 3 cm (1¼ inch) cubes
275 g (10 oz) tin bamboo shoots in water,
    drained, cut into matchsticks
50 g (2 oz) galangal, finely sliced
5 makrut (kaffir) lime leaves, torn in half
a handful of Thai sweet basil leaves,
    for garnish
1 long red chilli, seeded and finely sliced,
    for garnish

Serves 4

Put the coconut cream in a wok or saucepan and simmer over a medium heat for about 5 minutes, or until the cream separates and a layer of oil forms on the surface. Stir the cream if it starts to brown around the edges. Add the curry paste, stir well to combine and cook until fragrant.

Stir in the coconut milk, then add the sugar and fish sauce and cook for 2 to 3 minutes. Add the fish and bamboo shoots and simmer for about 5 minutes, stirring occasionally, until the fish is cooked.

Add the galangal and makrut lime leaves. Taste, then adjust the seasoning if necessary. Spoon onto a serving plate and sprinkle with the basil leaves and sliced chilli.

red curry with fish
and bamboo shoots

green curry
with fish balls

350 g (12 oz) white fish fillets, without
    skin and bone, roughly cut into pieces
60 ml (¼ cup) coconut cream
2 tablespoons green curry paste
    (page 244) or bought paste
440 ml (1¾ cups) coconut milk
350 g (12 oz) mixed Thai eggplants
    (aubergines), quartered, and pea
    eggplants (aubergines)
2 tablespoons fish sauce
2 tablespoons palm sugar
50 g (2 oz) galangal, finely sliced
3 makrut (kaffir) lime leaves, torn in half
a handful of holy basil leaves, for garnish
½ long red chilli, seeded and finely sliced,
    for garnish

Serves 4

In a food processor or a blender, chop the fish fillets into a smooth paste.
(If you have a pestle and mortar, pound the fish paste for another 10 minutes
to give it a chewy texture.)

Put the coconut cream in a wok or saucepan and simmer over a medium heat
for about 5 minutes, or until the cream separates and a layer of oil forms on
the surface. Stir the cream if it starts to brown around the edges. Add the
curry paste, stir well to combine and cook until fragrant. Add nearly all of the
coconut milk and mix well.

Use a spoon or your wet hands to shape the fish paste into small balls or
discs, about 2 cm (¾ inch) across, and drop them into the coconut milk. Add
the eggplants, fish sauce and sugar and cook for 12 to 15 minutes, stirring
occasionally, until the fish and eggplants are cooked.

Stir in the galangal and makrut lime leaves. Taste, then adjust the seasoning
if necessary. Spoon into a serving bowl and sprinkle with the last bit of
coconut milk, basil leaves and sliced chilli.

450 g (1 lb) mixed fresh seafood such as prawns (shrimp), squid tubes, small scallops
2 tablespoons vegetable oil
3–4 garlic cloves, finely chopped
1 green capsicum (pepper), cut into bite-sized pieces
1 small onion, cut into thin slices
5 snake beans, cut into 2.5 cm (1 inch) pieces
1 cm (½ inch) piece of ginger, finely grated

4 bird's eye chillies, lightly bruised
1 tablespoon oyster sauce
½ tablespoon light soy sauce
¼ teaspoon sugar
1 long red chilli (optional), seeded and sliced diagonally
1–2 spring onions (scallions), thinly sliced
a few holy basil leaves, or coriander (cilantro) leaves, for garnish

Serves 4

Peel and devein the prawns and cut each prawn open along the back so it opens like a butterfly (leave each prawn joined along the base and at the tail). Peel off the outer skin of the squid and rinse out the insides of the tubes. Cut each in half and open the pieces out. Score the inside of each squid with diagonal cuts to make a diamond pattern, then cut into squares. Carefully slice off and discard any vein, membrane or hard white muscle from each scallop. Scallops can be left whole or, if large, cut each in half.

Heat the oil in a wok or frying pan and stir-fry the garlic over a medium heat until light brown. Add the capsicum, onion, beans, ginger and chillies and stir-fry for 1 minute.

Add the seafood in stages, prawns first, then scallops, adding the squid last and tossing after each addition. Add the oyster sauce, light soy sauce and sugar and stir-fry for 2 to 3 minutes, or until the prawns open and turn pink and all the seafood is cooked.

Add the chilli and spring onions and toss together. Taste, then adjust the seasoning if necessary. Spoon onto a serving plate and sprinkle with basil or coriander leaves.

mixed seafood
with chillies

hot and sour soup with mixed seafood

600 g (1 lb 5 oz) mixed fresh seafood
   such as raw prawns (shrimp), squid
   tubes, mussels, white fish fillets and
   scallops
1 litre (4 cups) vegetable stock
3 x 4 cm (1½ inch) lemon grass stalks,
   white part only, each cut into a tassel
   or bruised
6 coriander (cilantro) roots, bruised
2–2½ tablespoons fish sauce
1½–2 tablespoons Chiang Mai curry paste
   (page 249), according to taste,
   or 2 dried red chillies, soaked, drained
   and finely chopped

2–3 bird's eye chillies, bruised
2 Asian shallots, smashed with the flat
   side of a cleaver
110 g (4 oz) straw or mixed mushrooms,
   left whole if small, or quartered if large
150 g (5 oz) baby tomatoes (about 12,
   cut in half if large) or medium tomatoes,
   each cut into 6 pieces
8 makrut (kaffir) lime leaves, torn
3 tablespoons lime juice

Serves 4

Peel and devein the prawns and cut each prawn along the back so it opens like a butterfly (leave each prawn joined along the base and at the tail).

Peel off any skin from the squid tubes, rinse the insides and cut the tubes into 5 mm (¼ inch) rings. If the squid are very big, cut them in half, open the tubes and slightly score the inside of each squid with diagonal cuts to make a diamond pattern. Cut the tubes into pieces about 2 cm (¾ inch) square. Remove any dark veins from the scallops.

Scrub the mussels and remove their hairy beards. Discard any open mussels and any that don't close when tapped on the work surface. Cut the fish into 2 cm (¾ inch) cubes.

Put the stock, lemon grass, coriander roots, fish sauce, curry paste and chillies in a large saucepan and bring to a boil.

Reduce the heat to medium, add the seafood and cook for 2 to 3 minutes. (If using cooked mussels, add them after the tomatoes.) Add the shallots, mushrooms, baby tomatoes, makrut lime leaves and cook for 2 to 3 minutes, taking care not to let the tomatoes lose their shape. Taste, add the lime juice, then adjust the seasoning if necessary. Spoon into a serving bowl.

a little taste of...

Thailand is rich in fresh vegetables — farmed commercially in the warm climate, grown on a small scale in vegetable gardens or picked wild, water spinach and lotus roots flourishing alongside the waterways. Much is eaten at home, while extra farm produce is brought daily by truck or flat-bottomed boat into the city markets.

Unusually in Asia, the Thais enjoy eating raw vegetables. The chilli dip, *naam phrik*, is served with the Thai equivalent of crudités — slivers of cucumber or cabbage — while the whole point of Thai salads, *yam*, is the absolute freshness of the crisp raw ingredients contrasted with the sweet, salty, sour dressing.

Despite the majority being Buddhists, very few Thais are actually vegetarian. Instead most observe a distinction between killing an animal themselves and eating it, with fishing deemed perfectly acceptable by all except the most devout. However, the Thais have never been great meat-eaters or hunters. In such a fertile environment food is easily foraged from the land, rivers and sea, so protein is more likely to come in the form of fish, small birds and insects, with tofu (bean curd) and nuts adding goodness to the vegetable-loaded diet.

...the vegetable garden

12 small round Thai eggplants
   (aubergines), green, yellow or purple
1 teaspoon fish sauce, plus 1 tablespoon
1 tablespoon vegetable oil
1 small red chilli, chopped
1 tablespoon finely sliced ginger
2 Asian shallots, finely chopped
1 garlic clove, chopped
150 g (5 oz) cherry tomatoes
2 tablespoons black vinegar
2 tablespoons palm sugar
12–18 Thai sweet basil leaves

Serves 4

Cut each eggplant in half and toss them in a bowl with 1 teaspoon fish sauce. Put about 8 cm (3 inches) of water in a wok and bring to the boil. Place the eggplants in a bamboo steamer, place the steamer over the boiling water and steam the eggplants for 15 minutes.

Heat the oil in a wok, add the chilli, ginger, shallots and garlic and cook for 15 seconds. Add the eggplants and tomatoes and toss well. Add the black vinegar, sugar and remaining fish sauce and cook for 2 to 3 minutes, until the sauce thickens. Stir in the basil leaves and serve.

baby eggplant and cherry tomato stir-fry

fragrant tofu and tomato soup

PASTE
½ teaspoon dried shrimp paste
1 teaspoon small dried prawns (shrimp)
4 Asian shallots, roughly chopped
½ teaspoon white peppercorns
2 coriander (cilantro) roots
1 garlic clove, chopped
2 teaspoons grated ginger

1 tablespoon vegetable oil
750 ml (3 cups) chicken stock or water
3 tablespoons tamarind purée
1 tablespoon palm sugar

2 tablespoons fish sauce
3 cm (1¼ inch) piece of ginger, julienned
3 Asian shallots, smashed with the flat
 side of a cleaver
300 g (10 oz) silken tofu (bean curd),
 cut into 2 cm (¾ inch) cubes
2 tomatoes, each cut into 8 wedges
1 tablespoon lime juice
2 tablespoons coriander (cilantro) leaves,
 for garnish

Serves 4

To make the paste, use a pestle and mortar or food processor to pound or blend the shrimp paste, dried prawns, shallots, peppercorns, coriander roots, garlic and ginger together.

Heat the oil in a saucepan over a low heat, add the paste and cook for 10 to 15 seconds, stirring constantly. Add the stock or water, tamarind purée, palm sugar, fish sauce and ginger. Simmer for 5 minutes to soften the ginger.

Add the shallots, tofu, tomatoes and lime juice to the saucepan and cook for 2 to 3 minutes to heat through. Garnish with coriander leaves.

2 large eggs
2 teaspoons light soy sauce
1 spring onion (scallion), finely sliced
a pinch of ground white pepper
1½ tablespoons vegetable oil
3–4 garlic cloves, finely chopped
a few coriander (cilantro) leaves,
    for garnish
1–2 long red chillies, thinly sliced,
    for garnish

Serves 2

Beat the eggs in a bowl with a fork. Mix in 170 ml (²/₃ cup) water and the soy sauce, spring onion and pepper. Divide evenly between two small heatproof bowls.

Fill a wok or steamer pan with water, cover, bring to a boil, then reduce the heat to medium. Taking care not to burn your hands, place the bowls on the rack of a bamboo steaming basket or on a steamer rack in the wok or pan. Cover the steamer and leave over the simmering water for 13 to 15 minutes or until the eggs set. Test with a skewer or fork. If it comes out clean the eggs are cooked.

Heat the oil and stir-fry the garlic until golden. Serve the eggs hot or warm, sprinkled with the garlic. Garnish with coriander leaves and chillies.

steamed eggs

stir-fried mixed vegetables

4 thin asparagus spears
4 baby sweet corn
50 g (2 oz) snake beans
110 g (4 oz) mixed red and yellow
    capsicums (peppers)
½ small carrot
50 g (2 oz) Chinese broccoli or broccoli
    florets
25 g (1 oz) snow peas (mangetout),
    topped and tailed
2 cm (¾ inch) piece of ginger, finely
    sliced
1 tablespoon fish sauce
1½ tablespoons oyster sauce
2 tablespoons vegetable stock or water
½ teaspoon sugar
1½ tablespoons vegetable oil
3–4 garlic cloves, finely chopped
2 spring onions (scallions), sliced

Serves 4

Cut off the tips of the asparagus and slice each spear into 5 cm (2 inch) lengths. Cut the sweet corn in halves lengthways and the beans into 2.5 cm (1 inch) lengths. Cut both on an angle. Halve the capsicums and remove the seeds, then cut into bite-sized pieces. Peel the carrot and cut into batons.

Blanch the asparagus stalks, sweet corn, beans and broccoli florets in boiling salted water for 30 seconds. Remove and place in a bowl of iced water to ensure a crispy texture. Drain and place in a bowl with the capsicum, carrot, snow peas, asparagus tips and ginger.

Mix the fish sauce, oyster sauce, stock and sugar in a small bowl.

Heat the oil in a wok or frying pan and stir-fry the garlic over a medium heat until light brown. Add the mixed vegetables and the sauce mixture, then stir-fry over a high heat for 2 to 3 minutes. Taste, then adjust the seasoning if necessary. Add the spring onions and toss.

**350 g (12 oz) Chinese broccoli,
  cut into pieces**
1 tablespoon vegetable oil
2 garlic cloves, finely chopped
1 tablespoon oyster sauce
1 tablespoon light soy sauce

Serves 4

Blanch the Chinese broccoli in boiling salted water for 2 to 3 minutes, then drain thoroughly.

Heat the oil in a wok or frying pan and stir-fry the garlic over a medium heat until light brown. Add the Chinese broccoli and half of the oyster sauce and the light soy sauce. Stir-fry over a high heat for 1 to 2 minutes until the stems are just tender. Drizzle with the remaining oyster sauce.

stir-fried broccoli with oyster sauce

coriander, basil and mint...

One of the most distinctive aspects of Thai cooking is its use of fresh herbs. Herbs certainly contribute flavour — handfuls tossed into dishes like a vegetable to give a pungent essence — but in a cuisine where presentation is as important as taste, the appearance and aroma of fresh herbs is by no means secondary.

In most Thai recipes, coriander (cilantro) is the essential herb. Unusually, it is the roots that are prized for their aroma and heady taste, pounded with garlic, salt and peppercorns as a foundation for many dishes. The refreshing leaves and stems are added to almost all soups, salads and fish dishes.

Thai cooks also use three varieties of basil, all quite different from European basil. Thai sweet basil has a basic flavour, its aniseed pungency sweetening soups and red and yellow curries. The strong aroma of Holy basil, sometimes called 'hot basil' because of its peppery spiciness, is accentuated when cooked and used only in strong dishes. There is also a delicate lemon basil thrown into soups and seafood. Spearmint is added fresh to seafood or minced meat salads, its cool fragrance and taste a contrast to the chilli-heat of these dishes.

pumpkin with chilli and basil

3 tablespoons dried shrimp
½ teaspoon shrimp paste
2 coriander (cilantro) roots
10–12 white peppercorns
2 garlic cloves, chopped
2 Asian shallots, chopped
125 ml (½ cup) coconut cream
300 g (10 oz) butternut pumpkin (squash),
  cut into 4 cm (1½ inch) cubes
2 large red chillies, cut lengthways
125 ml (½ cup) coconut milk
1 tablespoon fish sauce
1 tablespoon palm sugar
2 teaspoons lime juice
12 Thai sweet basil leaves

Serves 4

Soak 2 tablespoons of the dried shrimp in a small bowl of water for about 20 minutes, then drain.

Put the remaining dried shrimp, shrimp paste, coriander roots, peppercorns, garlic and shallots in a pestle and mortar or food processor and pound or blend to a paste.

Bring the coconut cream to a boil in a saucepan and simmer for 5 minutes. Add the paste and stir to combine. Cook for another 2 to 3 minutes, then add the pumpkin, chillies, rehydrated shrimp and coconut milk. Stir to combine all the ingredients and simmer for 10 to 15 minutes, until the pumpkin is just tender. Don't let the pumpkin turn to mush.

Add the fish sauce, palm sugar and lime juice to the pan and cook for another 2 to 3 minutes. Stir in the basil leaves before serving.

1 dried long red chilli
1 lemon grass stalk, white part only, finely sliced
4 Asian shallots, finely chopped
2–3 garlic cloves, roughly chopped
½ teaspoon shrimp paste
1½ tablespoons vegetable oil
175 g (6 oz) minced (ground) fatty pork
450 g (1 lb) tomatoes, finely chopped
2 tablespoons fish sauce
1 tablespoon sugar

3 tablespoons tamarind purée
mixed vegetables, such as wedges of eggplant (aubergine), pieces of snake bean, wedges of cabbage, asparagus spears, baby corn, pieces of pumpkin, to serve
a few coriander (cilantro) leaves, for garnish
pieces of pork skin, deep-fried, to serve

Serves 4

Slit the chilli lengthways with a sharp knife and discard all the seeds. Soak the chilli in hot water for 1 to 2 minutes or until soft, then drain and chop roughly. Using a pestle and mortar, pound the chilli, lemon grass, shallots and garlic into a paste. Add the shrimp paste and mix well. Alternatively, use a small processor or blender to grind or blend the chilli, lemon grass, shallots, garlic and shrimp paste into a smooth paste.

Heat the oil in a saucepan or wok and stir-fry the paste over a medium heat for 2 minutes or until fragrant. Add the minced pork and stir for 2 to 3 minutes. Add the tomatoes, fish sauce, sugar and tamarind. Reduce the heat and gently simmer for 25 to 30 minutes or until the mixture is thick.

Blanch briefly any tough vegetables such as eggplant, snake beans, asparagus and pumpkin. Drain well.

Taste the sauce, then adjust with more tamarind, sugar or chilli if necessary. This dish should have three flavours: sweet, sour and lightly salted. Spoon into a serving bowl and garnish with coriander leaves. Serve with a mixture of blanched vegetables and deep-fried pork skin.

spicy tomato
dipping sauce

wing bean salad

oil, for frying
75 g (3 oz) Asian shallots, finely sliced
175 g (6 oz) wing beans
55 g (2 oz) cooked chicken, shredded
1 lemon grass stalk, white part only,
    finely sliced
2 tablespoons dried shrimp, ground
1½ tablespoons fish sauce
3–4 tablespoons lime juice
½ long red chilli or 1 small red chilli, finely
    chopped
55 g (2 oz) whole salted roasted peanuts
125 ml (½ cup) coconut milk, for garnish

Serves 4

Heat 2.5 cm (1 inch) oil in a wok or deep frying pan over a medium heat. Deep-fry the shallots for 3 to 4 minutes until they are light brown (without burning them). Lift out with a slotted spoon and drain on paper towels.

Slice the wing beans diagonally into thin pieces. Blanch the wing beans in boiling water for 30 seconds, then drain and put them in cold water for 1 to 2 minutes. Drain and transfer to a bowl. Add the cooked chicken, lemon grass, dried shrimp, fish sauce, lime juice, chilli and half the peanuts. Mix with a spoon. Taste, then adjust the seasoning if necessary.

Put the wing bean salad in a serving bowl, drizzle with coconut milk and sprinkle with the crispy shallots and the rest of the peanuts.

350 g (12 oz) firm tofu (bean curd)
1 teaspoon sesame oil
2 teaspoons light soy sauce
¼ teaspoon ground black pepper,
   plus some to sprinkle
1 tablespoon finely shredded ginger
5 tablespoons vegetable stock or water
2 tablespoons light soy sauce
2 teaspoons cornflour (cornstarch)
½ teaspoon sugar
1½ tablespoons vegetable oil
2 garlic cloves, finely chopped
200 g (7 oz) oyster mushrooms, hard
   stalks removed, cut in half if large
200 g (7 oz) shiitake mushrooms, hard
   stalks removed
2 spring onions (scallions), sliced
   diagonally, for garnish
1 long red chilli, seeded and finely sliced,
   for garnish

Serves 2

Drain each block of tofu and cut into 2.5 cm (1 inch) pieces. Put them in a shallow dish and sprinkle with the sesame oil, light soy sauce, ground pepper and ginger. Leave to marinate for 30 minutes.

Mix the stock with the light soy sauce, cornflour and sugar in a small bowl until smooth.

Heat the oil in a wok or frying pan and stir-fry the garlic over a medium heat until light brown. Add all the mushrooms and stir-fry for 3 to 4 minutes or until the mushrooms are cooked. Add the cornflour liquid, then carefully add the pieces of tofu and gently mix for 1 to 2 minutes. Taste, then adjust the seasoning if necessary.

Spoon onto a serving plate and sprinkle with spring onions, chilli slices and ground pepper.

mushrooms with tofu

son-in-law eggs

2 dried long red chillies, about 13 cm
   (5 inches) long
vegetable oil, for deep-frying
110 g (4 oz) Asian shallots, finely sliced
6 large hard-boiled eggs, shelled
2 tablespoons fish sauce
3 tablespoons tamarind purée
5 tablespoons palm sugar

Serves 4

Cut the chillies into 5 mm (¼ inch) pieces with scissors or a knife and discard the seeds. Heat 5 cm (2 inches) oil in a wok or deep frying pan over a medium heat. When the oil seems hot, drop a slice of the Asian shallot into the oil. If it sizzles straight away, the oil is ready. Deep-fry the chillies for a few seconds, being careful not to burn them, to bring out the flavour. Remove them with a slotted spoon, then drain on paper towels.

In the same wok, deep-fry the Asian shallots for 3 to 4 minutes until golden brown. Be careful not to burn them. Remove with a slotted spoon, then drain on paper towels. Use a spoon to slide one egg at a time into the same hot oil. Be careful as the oil may splash. Deep-fry for 10 to 15 minutes or until the whole of each egg is golden brown. Remove with a slotted spoon, then drain on paper towels. Keep warm.

In a saucepan over a medium heat, stir the fish sauce, tamarind purée and sugar for 5 to 7 minutes or until all the sugar has dissolved.

Halve the eggs lengthways and arrange them with the yolk upwards on a serving plate. Drizzle the tamarind sauce over the eggs and sprinkle the crispy chillies and shallots over them.

2 tablespoons oyster sauce
1 tablespoon light soy sauce
1 teaspoon sugar
2 tablespoons vegetable oil
4 garlic cloves, finely chopped
225 g (8 oz) mixed vegetables
   (Chinese broccoli florets, baby sweet
   corn, snake beans cut into lengths,
   snow peas/mangetout), cut into
   bite-sized pieces
250 g (9 oz) fresh egg noodles
45 g (½ cup) bean sprouts
3 spring onions (scallions), finely chopped
½ long red or green chilli, seeded and
   finely sliced
a few coriander (cilantro) leaves,
   for garnish

Serves 4

Combine the oyster sauce, light soy sauce and sugar in a small bowl.

Heat the oil in a wok or frying pan and stir-fry the garlic over a medium heat until lightly browned. Add all the mixed vegetables and stir-fry over a high heat for 1 to 2 minutes.

Add the egg noodles and oyster sauce mixture to the wok and stir-fry for 2 to 3 minutes. Add the bean sprouts and spring onions. Taste, then adjust the seasoning if necessary.

Spoon onto a serving plate and garnish with chilli and coriander leaves.

stir-fried egg noodles
with vegetables

a little taste of...

Although just about all cuisines treasure sweets, puddings following the meal are largely a western culinary notion. In Thailand, their pretty desserts, *khwang waan*, are more likely to be eaten as a snack on the street than served to finish off a meal. Rarely made at home, a vendor's speciality is piled up onto their pushcart, the mound of banana-leaf wrapped sticky rice, coconut custards or triangles of fruit jellies are all rich, filling and meant to satisfy hunger. If anything sweet is served at the end of a meal, it is usually a plate of fruit, often with a little salt added. At a formal meal, two desserts may be offered, a wet and a dry one, the liquid one often combining fruit and coconut; the dry, *kanom*, usually little cakes or jellies.

The Thais don't really use any dairy products or chocolate in their cooking and the flavours of their sweets can seem quite unusual, with most made from sticky rice, coconut, tapioca, fruit and palm sugar. Thai confectioners strive for the same layers of textures and balance of sweet, salty and sour that underlies all Thai cooking — soft, sweet fruit partnered with salty coconut rice.

...sweets

sticky rice with mango

4 large ripe mangoes
1 quantity of steamed sticky rice with
  coconut milk (page 243)
170 ml (²/₃ cup) coconut cream mixed with
  ¼ teaspoon salt, for garnish
2 tablespoons dry-fried mung beans
  (optional)

Serves 4

Peel the mangoes and slice off the two outside cheeks of each, removing as much flesh as you can in large pieces. Avoid cutting very close to the stone where the flesh is fibrous. Discard the stone. Slice each cheek lengthways into four or five pieces.

Arrange the mango pieces on a serving plate. Spoon a portion of steamed sticky rice with coconut milk near the mango slices. Spoon the coconut cream garnish on top and sprinkle with mung beans. Serve at room temperature.

410 ml (1²/₃ cups) coconut milk
250 ml (1 cup) thick (double/heavy)
  cream
2 eggs
4 egg yolks
160 g (²/₃ cup) caster (superfine) sugar
¼ teaspoon salt

Serves 10

Pour the coconut milk and cream into a medium saucepan. Stir over a gentle heat without boiling for 2 to 3 minutes. Remove from the heat, cover and keep warm over a bowl of boiling water.

Put the eggs, egg yolks, sugar and salt in a large heatproof bowl. Beat the mixture with electric beaters for 3 minutes or until frothy and thickened.

Place the bowl over a pan of simmering water. Continue to beat the egg mixture, slowly adding all the coconut mixture until the custard thickens lightly. This process will take 8 to 10 minutes. The mixture should be a thin cream and easily coat the back of a spoon. Do not boil it or it will curdle. Set aside until cool. Stir the mixture occasionally while it is cooling. Pour into a freezer box or churn in an ice cream machine. If you are using a freezer box, take the mixture out of the freezer and beat it with electric beaters at least twice during the freezing. You want it to get plenty of air whipped into it. Cover and freeze completely.

To serve, remove from the freezer for 10 to 15 minutes until slightly softened, then serve in scoops. Delicious with slices of coconut.

coconut ice cream

banana in
coconut cream

410 ml (1²/₃ cups) coconut milk
4 tablespoons sugar
5 just-ripe bananas
¹/₂ teaspoon salt

Serves 4

Put the coconut milk, sugar and 125 ml (¹/₂ cup) water in a saucepan and bring to a boil. Reduce the heat and simmer until the sugar dissolves.

Peel the bananas and cut them into 5 cm (2 inch) lengths. If you are using very small bananas, leave them whole.

When the sugar in the coconut milk has dissolved, add the bananas and salt. Cook gently over a low to medium heat for 5 minutes or until the bananas are soft.

Divide the bananas and coconut cream among four bowls. Serve warm or at room temperature

banana leaves
80 ml (⅓ cup) coconut milk
7 eggs
275 g (10 oz) palm sugar, cut into
   very small pieces
¼ teaspoon salt
5–6 fresh pandanus leaves, dried
   and cut into small pieces, bruised,
   or 3 teaspoons vanilla essence

100 g (3½ oz) young coconut meat,
   cut into small pieces, or orange sweet
   potato, jackfruit or taro, cut into
   matchsticks

Makes 6

To **soften** the banana leaves and prevent them from splitting, put them in a hot oven for about 10 seconds, or blanch them briefly. Cut the banana leaves into 12 circles about 13 cm (5 inches) in diameter with the fibre running lengthways. Place one piece with the fibre running lengthways and another on top of it with the fibre running across. Make a 1 cm (½ inch) tuck 4 cm (1½ inches) long (4 cm in from the edge and no further) and pin securely with a small sharp toothpick. Repeat this at the opposite point and at the two side points, making four tucks altogether. Flatten the base as best you can. Repeat to make 6 square-shaped cups. Alternatively, use a small shallow rectangular tin such as a brownie tin.

Combine the coconut milk, eggs, sugar, salt and pandanus leaves in a bowl, using a spoon, for 10 minutes or until the sugar has dissolved. Pour the custard through the sieve into a bowl to discard the pandanus leaves.

Add the coconut, orange sweet potato, taro or jackfruit to the custard and lightly mix. Spoon the mixture into each banana cup, filling to within 1 cm (½ inch) from the top.

Half fill a wok or a steamer pan with water, cover and bring to a rolling boil over a high heat. Place the banana cups on a plate. Use a plate that will fit on the rack of a traditional bamboo steamer basket or on a steamer rack inside the wok or pan. Taking care not to burn your hands, place the plate on the bamboo steamer or steamer rack inside the wok or pan. Cover, reduce the heat to low and cook for 10 to 15 minutes. Check and replenish the water after 10 minutes. Serve at room temperature or chilled. The custards can be covered and refrigerated for up to 3 to 4 days.

custards

the coconut... As the Thais eat almost no dairy products, the creaminess of their savoury dishes and butteriness of their rich sweets comes instead from the coconut, a fruit available to all and scattered with abundance across the length and breadth of the country.

The coconut is one of the most versatile of foods. Unusually, Thai cooking doesn't make much use of animal fats so coconut cream, the main source of fat in the Thai diet, also replaces oil or butter in many recipes. Curry pastes and fresh seasonings are cooked in the oil that separates out from the heated cream, then meat, poultry, seafood or vegetables are added to the soupy mix.

Fresh coconut cream is not in fact the liquid found inside the nut, but is made from grated coconut meat steeped in hot water and 'milked' to produce a liquid with a rich, thick consistency. This cream contains little water so that it can be cooked to a high temperature. Its thinner relation, coconut milk, is taken from a second soaking. The coconut meat is also grated for cooking, while hawkers sell thirst-quenching chilled coconut water in the husks of green coconuts.

mango sorbet

3 ripe mangoes
150 g (5½ oz) palm sugar
zest and juice from 1 lime

Serves 4

Peel the mangoes and cut the flesh off the stones. Chop into small pieces. Put the sugar and 185 ml (¾ cup) water in a saucepan and bring to the boil. Reduce the heat and simmer until the liquid reduces by half. Put the sugar syrup, mango and lime zest and juice in a food processor or blender and whiz until smooth.

Pour into a freezer box or churn in an ice cream machine. If you are using a freezer box, take the mixture out of the freezer and beat it with electric beaters at least twice during the freezing time. You want it to have plenty of air whipped into it or the sorbet will be too icy and hard. Cover and freeze completely.

175 g (6 oz) black sticky rice (black glutinous)
280 g (10 oz) taro, cut into 1 cm (½ inch) squares and soaked in cold water
150 g (5 oz) palm sugar
1 teaspoon salt
185 ml (¾ cup) coconut milk

Serves 6

Put the rice in a bowl and pour in cold water to come 5 cm (2 inches) above the rice. Soak for at least 3 hours, or overnight if possible.

Drain the rice and add clean water. Scoop the rice through your fingers four or five times to clean it, then drain. Repeat two or three times with clean water to remove the unwanted starch. (The water will never be completely clear when using black rice, even when all the unwanted starch has gone.) Put the rice in a saucepan and add 625 ml (2½ cups) cold water.

Bring to the boil, stirring the rice frequently as it reaches boiling point. Reduce the heat to medium. Stir and simmer for 30 to 35 minutes or until nearly all the liquid has been absorbed. The rice should be very moist, but with hardly any water remaining in the bottom of the saucepan. (Taste a few grains to check whether the rice is cooked.)

Meanwhile, drain the taro, spread it on a plate and transfer it to a bamboo steamer or other steamer. Taking care not to burn your hands, set the basket over a pan of boiling water over a high heat. Cover and steam for about 8 to 10 minutes or until the taro is cooked and tender.

When the rice is cooked, add the sugar and gently stir until the sugar has dissolved. Add the taro and gently mix.

Mix the salt into the coconut milk. Divide the pudding among individual bowls and drizzle coconut milk on top. Serve warm.

black sticky rice with taro

deep-fried bananas

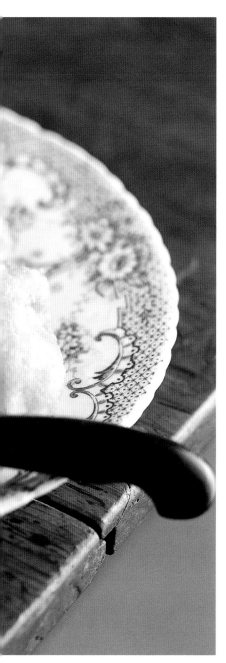

BATTER
125 g (1 cup) self-raising flour
½ teaspoon baking powder
2 teaspoons sugar
¼ teaspoon salt
25 g (1 oz) grated coconut or desiccated
 coconut
2 tablespoons sesame seeds
350 ml (1⅓ cups) water, at room
 temperature

vegetable oil, for deep-frying
4 ripe bananas

Serves 4

Put the flour, baking powder, sugar, salt, coconut and sesame seeds in a bowl. Add the water and lightly mix with a spoon or fork until smooth.

Heat 7.5 cm (3 inches) oil in a wok or deep-frying pan over a medium heat. When the oil seems hot, drop a little batter into the oil. If it sizzles immediately, the oil is ready. It is important not to have the oil too hot or the batter will burn.

Halve the bananas lengthways, then cut them into 5 cm (2 inch) chunks. Preheat the oven to 150°C/300°F/Gas 2. Dip the banana chunks one at a time into the batter, then lower into the hot oil. Deep-fry about 5 pieces at a time for 3 to 4 minutes or until golden, then lift out with a slotted spoon or a pair of chopsticks. Drain on paper towels and keep warm in the oven. Transfer to a serving plate and serve warm.

2 tablespoons coconut milk

2 eggs

150 g (5 oz) palm sugar, cut or shaved
　into very small pieces

2–3 pandanus leaves, dried and cut into
　small pieces, and bruised, or 1 teaspoon
　vanilla essence

1 small to medium or 4 very small
　pumpkins

Serves 4

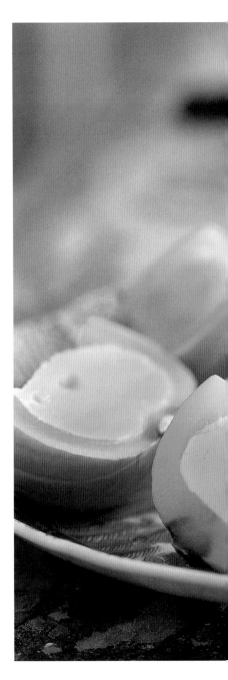

To make a custard, stir the coconut milk, eggs, palm sugar, pandanus leaves
and a pinch of salt in a bowl, using a spoon, for 10 minutes or until the
sugar has dissolved. Pour the custard through a sieve into a jug to discard
the pandanus leaves.

Carefully cut off the top of the pumpkin/s. Try not to pierce the pumpkin at
any other point with the knife as it is more likely to crack or leak around such
punctures. Using a spoon, scrape out and discard all the seeds and fibres.

Fill a wok or a steamer pan with water, cover and bring to a rolling boil over
a high heat. Place the pumpkin/s on a plate. Use a plate that will fit on the
rack of a traditional bamboo steamer basket or on a steamer rack inside the
wok. Taking care not to burn your hands, place the plate on the rack or
steamer inside the wok. Pour the custard into the pumpkin/s, filling to within
2.5 cm (1 inch) from the top. Cover, reduce the heat to low and cook for
about 30 to 45 minutes or until the pumpkin is cooked and the custard puffed
up. Check and replenish the water every 10 minutes or so.

Turn off the heat and remove the cover. Carefully remove the pumpkin and
set aside to cool. If you prefer, you can leave the pumpkin in the steamer to
cool to room temperature. Cut the pumpkin into thick wedges for serving.
Serve at room temperature or chilled.

As an alternative, you can steam the mixture in a shallow tin, such as a pie
tin or cake pan, and serve it in small spoonfuls on top of mounds of steamed
sticky rice with coconut milk.

pumpkin with custard

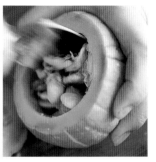

basics

STEAMED RICE

400 g (2 cups) jasmine rice

Serves 4

Rinse the rice until the water runs clear. Put the rice in a saucepan and add enough water to come an index-finger joint above the rice. Bring to the boil, cover and cook at a slow simmer for 10 to 15 minutes. Remove from the heat and leave it to rest for 10 minutes before serving.

STICKY RICE

400 g (2 cups) sticky rice

Serves 4

Put the rice in a bowl and pour in cold water to come 5 cm (2 inches) above the rice. Soak for at least 3 hours, or overnight. Drain and transfer to a bamboo basket specially made for steaming sticky rice, or to a steamer lined with a double thickness of muslin. Spread the rice in the steamer. Bring the water in the bottom of the steamer to a rolling boil. Taking care, set the rice over the water. Lower the heat, cover and steam for 20 to 25 minutes or until the rice swells and is glistening and tender. The cooking time will vary depending on the soaking time. Check and replenish the water every 10 minutes or so.

When the rice is cooked, tip it onto a large tray and spread it out to help it cool quickly. If it cools slowly it will be soggy rather than sticky. Serve warm or cold.

STEAMED STICKY RICE WITH COCONUT MILK

200 g (1 cup) sticky rice
170 ml (²/₃ cup) coconut milk, well stirred
1 tablespoon palm sugar (not too brown)
½ teaspoon salt

Serves 4

Cook the sticky rice according to the instructions in the recipe above.

While the rice is cooking, stir the coconut milk, sugar and salt in a small saucepan over low heat until the sugar has dissolved. As soon as the rice is cooked, use a wooden spoon to gently mix it with the coconut milk. Set aside for 15 minutes.

GREEN CURRY PASTE

1 teaspoon ground coriander
1 teaspoon ground cumin
8–10 small green chillies, seeded
2 lemon grass stalks, white part only, finely sliced
2.5 cm (1 inch) piece of galangal, finely chopped
1 teaspoon very finely chopped makrut (kaffir) lime skin or
    makrut lime leaves (about half the skin from a makrut lime
    or 4–5 leaves)
4–5 garlic cloves, finely chopped
3–4 Asian shallots, chopped
5–6 coriander (cilantro) roots, finely chopped
a handful of holy basil leaves, finely chopped
2 teaspoons shrimp paste

Makes 125 g (½ cup)

Dry-roast the coriander in a small frying pan for 1 minute until fragrant, then remove from the pan. Repeat with the cumin.

Using a pestle and mortar, pound the chillies, lemon grass, galangal and makrut lime skin or leaves into a paste. Add the garlic, shallots and coriander roots and pound together. Add the remaining ingredients and dry-roasted spices one at a time and pound until the mixture forms a smooth paste.

Alternatively, you can use a food processor or blender to blend all the ingredients into as smooth a paste as possible. Add cooking oil as needed to assist the blending.

Use as required or keep in an airtight jar. The paste will keep for at least two weeks in the refrigerator and for two months in a freezer.

RED CURRY PASTE

3–4 dried long red chillies, about 13 cm (5 inches) long
8–10 dried small red chillies, about 5 cm (2 inches) long
    or 10 fresh small red chillies, seeded
2 lemon grass stalks, white part only, finely sliced
2.5 cm (1 inch) piece of galangal, finely sliced
1 teaspoon very finely chopped makrut (kaffir) lime skin or
    makrut lime leaves (about half the skin from a makrut lime
    or 4–5 leaves)
4–5 garlic cloves, finely chopped
3–4 Asian shallots, finely chopped
5–6 coriander (cilantro) roots, finely chopped
2 teaspoons shrimp paste
1 teaspoon ground coriander, dry-roasted

Makes 125 g (½ cup)

Remove the stems from the dried chillies and slit the chillies lengthways with a sharp knife. Discard the seeds and soak the chillies in hot water for 1 to 2 minutes or until soft. Drain and roughly chop.

Using a pestle and mortar, pound the chillies, lemon grass, galangal and makrut lime skin or leaves into a paste. Add the remaining ingredients and pound together until the mixture forms a smooth paste.

Alternatively, you can use a food processor or blender to blend all the ingredients into as smooth a paste as possible. Add cooking oil, as needed, to assist the blending.

Use as required or keep in an airtight jar. The paste will keep for at least two weeks in the refrigerator and for two months in a freezer.

YELLOW CURRY PASTE

3 teaspoons coriander seeds, dry-roasted
1 teaspoon cumin seeds, dry-roasted
2–3 dried long red chillies
2 lemon grass stalks, white part only,
**   finely sliced**
3 Asian shallots, finely chopped
2 garlic cloves, finely chopped
2 tablespoons grated turmeric or
**   1 teaspoon ground turmeric**
1 teaspoon shrimp paste

Makes 250 g (1 cup)

Grind the coriander seeds to a powder with a pestle and mortar, then grind the cumin seeds.

Remove the stems from the chillies and slit the chillies lengthways with a sharp knife. Discard the seeds and soak the chillies in hot water for 1 to 2 minutes or until soft. Drain and roughly chop.

Using a pestle and mortar, pound the chillies, lemon grass, shallots, garlic and turmeric to as smooth a paste as possible. Add the shrimp paste, ground coriander and ground cumin and pound until the mixture forms a smooth paste.

Alternatively, use a small processor or blender, and blend all the ingredients into a very smooth paste. Add cooking oil, as needed, to assist the blending.

Use as required or keep in an airtight jar. The paste will keep for at least two weeks in the refrigerator and for two months in a freezer.

MASSAMAN CURRY PASTE

2 dried long red chillies, about 13 cm (5 inches) long
1 lemon grass stalk, white part only, finely sliced
2.5 cm (1 inch) piece of galangal, finely chopped
5 cloves
10 cm (4 inch) piece of cinnamon stick, crushed
10 cardamom seeds
½ teaspoon freshly grated nutmeg
6 garlic cloves, finely chopped
4 Asian shallots, finely chopped
4–5 coriander (cilantro) roots, finely chopped
1 teaspoon shrimp paste

Makes 250 g (1 cup)

Remove the stems from the chillies and slit the chillies lengthways with a sharp knife. Discard the seeds and soak the chillies in hot water for 1 to 2 minutes or until soft. Drain and roughly chop.

Using a pestle and mortar, pound the chillies, lemon grass, galangal, cloves, cinnamon, cardamom seeds and nutmeg into a paste. Add the garlic, shallots and coriander roots. Pound and mix together. Add the shrimp paste and pound until the mixture is a smooth paste.

Alternatively, use a food processor or blender to grind or blend all the ingredients into as smooth a paste as possible. Add cooking oil, as needed, to assist the blending.

Use as required or keep in an airtight jar. The paste will keep for up to two weeks in the refrigerator and for two months in a freezer.

DRY CURRY PASTE

2 dried long red chillies, about 13 cm (5 inches) long
2 lemon grass stalks, white part only, finely sliced
2.5 cm (1 inch) piece of galangal, finely chopped
4–5 garlic cloves, finely chopped
3–4 Asian shallots, finely chopped
5–6 coriander (cilantro) roots, finely chopped
1 teaspoon shrimp paste
1 teaspoon ground cumin, dry-roasted
3 tablespoons unsalted peanuts, chopped

Makes 80 g (⅓ cup)

Remove the stems from the chillies and slit the chillies lengthways with a sharp knife. Discard the seeds and soak the chillies in hot water for 1 to 2 minutes or until soft. Drain and roughly chop.

Using a pestle and mortar, pound the chillies, lemon grass and galangal into a paste. Add the remaining ingredients one at a time and pound until the mixture forms a very smooth paste.

Alternatively, you can use a food processor or blender to blend all the ingredients together into as smooth a paste as possible. Add cooking oil, as needed, to assist the blending.

Use as required or keep in an airtight jar. The paste will keep for at least two weeks in the refrigerator and for two months in a freezer.

CHIANG MAI CURRY PASTE

1 tablespoon coriander seeds
2 teaspoons cumin seeds
2 dried long red chillies, about 13 cm (5 inches) long
½ teaspoon salt
5 cm (2 inch) piece of galangal, grated
1 lemon grass stalk, white part only, finely chopped
2 Asian shallots, chopped
2 garlic cloves, chopped
1 teaspoon grated turmeric or a pinch of ground turmeric
1 teaspoon shrimp paste
½ teaspoon ground cassia or cinnamon

Makes 185 g (¾ cup)

Dry-roast the coriander seeds in a small frying pan for 1 minute until fragrant, then remove from the pan. Repeat with the cumin seeds. Grind them both to a powder with a pestle and mortar.

Remove the stems from the chillies and slit the chillies lengthways with a sharp knife. Discard the seeds. Soak the chillies in hot water for 1 to 2 minutes or until soft. Drain and roughly chop.

Using a pestle and mortar, pound the chillies, salt, galangal, lemon grass, shallots, garlic and turmeric to as smooth a paste as possible. Add the shrimp paste, ground coriander, cumin and cassia and mix until the mixture forms a smooth paste.

Alternatively, use a small processor or blender to blend all the ingredients into a very smooth paste. Add a little cooking oil, as needed, to ease the blending.

CHILLI JAM

80 ml (⅓ cup) oil
2 Asian shallots, finely chopped
2 garlic cloves, finely chopped
40 g (1½ oz) dried chilli flakes
¼ teaspoon palm sugar

Makes 185 g (¾ cup)

Heat the oil in a small saucepan and fry the shallots and garlic until brown. Add the chilli flakes and palm sugar and stir well. Season with a pinch of salt. Use as a dipping sauce or accompaniment. The sauce can be stored in a jar in the refrigerator for several weeks.

ROASTED CHILLI SAUCE

oil, for frying
20 Asian shallots, sliced
10 garlic cloves, sliced
3 tablespoons dried shrimp
7 dried long red chillies, chopped
3 tablespoons tamarind purée or
**   3 tablespoons lime juice**
6 tablespoons palm sugar
1 teaspoon shrimp paste
salt or fish sauce, to taste

Makes 250 g (1 cup)

Heat the oil in a wok or saucepan. Fry the shallots and garlic together until golden, then transfer from the wok to a blender or food processor.

Fry the dried shrimp and chillies for 1 to 2 minutes, then add these to the blender along with the remaining ingredients. Add as much of the frying oil as necessary to make a paste that you can pour. Put the paste back in the clean saucepan and bring to a boil. Reduce the heat and simmer until thick. Be careful because if you overcook this you will end up with a caramelized lump. Season the sauce with salt or fish sauce. Chilli jam is used as base for recipes, especially stir-fries, as well as a seasoning or accompaniment. It will keep for several months in an airtight jar in the refrigerator.

PEANUT SAUCE

2 garlic cloves, crushed
4 Asian shallots, finely chopped
1 lemon grass stalk, white part only,
    finely chopped
2 teaspoons Thai curry powder
1 tablespoon tamarind purée
1 tablespoon chilli paste
160 g (1 cup) unsalted roasted peanuts,
    roughly chopped
375 ml (1½ cups) coconut milk
2 teaspoons palm sugar

Makes 375 g (1½ cups)

Heat 1 tablespoon vegetable oil in a saucepan and fry the garlic, Asian shallots and lemon grass for a minute. Add the Thai curry powder and stir until fragrant.

Add the remaining ingredients and bring slowly to the boil. Add enough boiling water to make a spoonable sauce and simmer for 2 minutes. Season with salt.

CUCUMBER RELISH

4 tablespoons rice vinegar
125 g (½ cup) sugar
1 small red chilli, seeded and chopped
1 teaspoon fish sauce
80 g (½ cup) peanuts, lightly roasted and roughly chopped
1 Lebanese (short) cucumber, unpeeled, seeded, finely diced

Makes 185 g (¾ cup)

Put the vinegar and sugar in a small saucepan with 125 ml (½ cup) of water. Bring to the boil, then reduce the heat and simmer for 5 minutes.

Allow to cool before stirring in the chilli, fish sauce, peanuts and cucumber.

glossary

Asian shallots Small reddish-purple shallots used in South-east Asia. French shallots can be used instead.

bamboo shoots The edible shoots of bamboo. Available fresh when in season, otherwise preserved in jars or tinned. Fresh shoots should be blanched if they are bitter.

banana leaves Large green leaves, which can be used as a wrapping (dip briefly in boiling water or put in a hot oven for 10 seconds to soften them before use) for foods, or to line plates. Young leaves are preferable. Available from Asian food shops.

basil There are three types of basil used in Thai cuisine. Thai sweet basil has purplish stems, green leaves and an aniseed aroma and flavour. It is used in curries, soups and stir-fries. Holy basil is either red or green with slightly pointed, variegated leaves, and is used in stir-fries and fish dishes. Lemon basil is also called mint basil. It is less common and is used in curries and stir-fries and as a condiment.

betel leaves Known also as piper leaves or wild tea leaves, these are not true betel but are a close relative. Baby spinach leaves can be used instead.

coconut cream This is made by soaking freshly grated coconut in boiling water and then squeezing out a thick, sweet liquid. It is available tinned. Coconut cream is sometimes 'cracked' in order to fry curry pastes. This means it is boiled until the water evaporates out and it separates into oil and solids.

coconut milk A thinner version of coconut cream, made as above but with more water or from a second pressing.

coriander (cilantro) Fresh coriander leaves are used both as an ingredient and as a colourful garnish. The roots (*raak phak chii*) are chopped or ground and used in curry pastes and sauces. Buy bunches that have healthy green leaves and avoid any that are yellowing.

coriander seeds (*met phak chii*) The round seeds of the coriander plant have a spicy aroma and are used in some curry pastes. To intensify the flavour, dry-roast the seeds until aromatic, before crushing them. Best freshly ground for each dish. Available whole or ground.

cumin seeds The elongated ridged seeds of a plant of the parsley family, these have a peppery, slightly bitter flavour and are used in some curry pastes. To intensify the flavour, dry-roast

the seeds before crushing them. Best freshly ground for each dish. Available whole or ground.

curry powder Usually bought ready-made in Thailand as it is not widely used except in a few stir-fries, marinades, sauces and in curry puffs.

dried fish Used extensively in Thai cuisine and a common roadside sight near the coast, dried fish is usually fried and crumbled and used in dips, salads and pastes.

dried shrimp These are either ground until they form a fine fluff or rehydrated and used whole. Look for dark pink ones.

fish sauce (*naam plaa*) Made from salted anchovy-like fish that are left to break down naturally in the heat, fish sauce is literally the liquid that is drained off. It is the main source of salt flavouring in Thai cooking and is also used as a condiment. It varies in quality. Look for Tiparos or Golden Boy brands. A fermented version (*naam plaa raa*) is used in the North and North-east.

galangal or galingale A rhizome, similar to ginger, used extensively in Thai cooking, usually in place of ginger. It is most famously used in *tom khaa kai*.

ketchap manis A thick, sweet soy sauce used as a flavouring.

mint Mint is used in salads such as *laap* as well as being served alongside salads and rice-noodle soups.

mushrooms Straw mushrooms are usually found tinned except in Asia. Replace them with oyster mushrooms if you need to. Shiitake are used both fresh and dried. Dried ones need to be soaked in boiling water before use.

palm sugar Palm sugar is made by boiling sugar palm sap until it turns into a granular paste. Sold in hard cakes of varying sizes or as a slightly softer version in tubs. Malaysian and Indonesian brands of palm sugar are darker in colour and stronger in flavour. Unrefined, soft brown sugar can be used instead.

pandanus leaves These long green leaves are shaped like blades and are used as a flavouring in desserts and sweets, as well as a wrapping for small parcels of food. Pandanus are also called screwpine. Essence can be bought in small bottles from speciality Asian food shops. Pandanus leaves are often sold frozen.

peppercorns Green peppercorns are used in curries. Dried white peppercorns are used as a seasoning and as a garnish but black pepper is seldom used.

pickled garlic Served as an accompaniment, pickled garlic has a sweet/sour flavour. Preserved as whole heads that can be used as they are.

pickled ginger Eaten as an accompaniment to curries and snacks. Buy ready-made from Asian food shops.

roasted chilli powder Both bird's eye and sky-pointing chillies are used to make chilli powder. Buy from Asian food shops or make your own by roasting and grinding whole chillies.

roasted chilli sauce This sauce is made from dried red chillies roasted in oil. It usually includes shrimp paste and palm sugar. Roasted chilli sauce comes in mild, medium and hot and is sold in jars and plastic pouches. Use as a flavouring and as a relish.

shrimp paste A strong smelling dark brownish-pink paste sold in small tubs that are usually sealed with wax. It is made from salted, fermented and dried shrimp. Buy a Thai version as those from other Asian countries vary. Used as it is or roasted first and refrigerated. This is very strong smelling and is a main ingredient in dips such as *naam phrik*.

soy sauce Both light soy sauce and dark soy are used in Thai cooking. The dark one is sweeter than Chinese-style soy sauce.

spring roll sheets Wheat and egg dough wrappers that can be bought from Asian food shops and some good supermarkets. Look in the refrigerator or freezer sections. Squares of filo pastry can also be used.

tamarind A fruit whose flesh is used as a souring agent. Usually bought as a dried cake or prepared as a purée, tamarind is actually a pod filled with seeds and a fibrous flesh. If you buy tamarind cake, then it must be soaked in hot water and then rubbed and squeezed to dissolve the pulp around the fibres. The fibres are then sieved out. Pulp is sold as purée or concentrate but is sometimes referred to as tamarind water in recipes. Freshly made tamarind water has a fresher, stronger flavour.

turmeric A rhizome like ginger and galangal. In Thailand turmeric comes in white and yellow varieties. The yellow type is often referred to as red and is used fresh in curry pastes. Dried, it adds a yellow colour to curries, particularly Northern *khao sawy*. The white type is often eaten raw as a vegetable accompaniment to *naam phrik*.

vinegar White coconut vinegar is the most common. Any mild white vinegar or, better still, rice vinegar can be used as a substitute.

won ton sheets These sheets or wrappers are available from the refrigerator or freezer cabinets of Asian food shops. Some are yellow and include egg in the pastry and others are white. Gow gee and gyoza wrappers can also be used.

yellow bean sauce This paste made of yellow soy beans adds a salty flavour to dishes.

index

Published in 2004 by Murdoch Books Pty Limited.
© Text, design, photography and illustrations Murdoch Books 2004.
All rights reserved. Reprinted 2005 (twice), 2006 (twice), 2007, 2008 (twice).

Chief Executive: Juliet Rogers
Publisher: Kay Scarlett

Creative Director: Marylouise Brammer
Design Concept: Vivien Valk
Designer: Alex Frampton
Food Editor: Lulu Grimes
Photographer: Alan Benson (location and recipes)
Additional Photography: Ian Hofstetter (recipes)
Stylist: Mary Harris
Additional Styling: Katy Holder
Stylist's Assistant: Wendy Quisumbing
Recipes: Oi Cheepchaiissara
Additional Recipes: Ross Dobson
Additional Text: Kay Halsey
Editorial Director: Diana Hill
Editor: Rachel Carter
Production: Monika Vidovic

National Library of Australia Cataloguing-in-Publication Data
A little taste of Thailand. Includes index.
ISBN 978 1 74045 361 5
1. Cookery, Thai. I. Title. 641.59593

PRINTED IN CHINA by Midas Printing (Asia) Ltd

Murdoch Books Australia
Pier 8/9, 23 Hickson Road,
Millers Point NSW 2000
Phone: 61 (0) 2 8220 2000
Fax: 61 (0) 2 8220 2558

Murdoch Books UK Ltd
Erico House, 6th Floor,
93-99 Upper Richmond Road,
Putney, London SW15 2TG
Phone: + 44 (0) 20 8785 5995
Fax: + 44 (0) 20 8785 5985

IMPORTANT: Those who might be at risk from the effects of salmonella food poisoning (the elderly, pregnant women, young children
and those suffering from immune deficiency diseases) should consult their GP with any concerns about eating raw eggs.